Tom Cole wore many [...]
crocodile hunter, stockma[...] [...]reaker,
station owner, buffalo hunt[...] [...] grower, to name
but a few.

He was born in England in 1906 but left when he was
seventeen, travelling to Australia in search of adventure.

His first job was as a station hand in Queensland and it
quickly gave him a taste for more. Before long Tom
was an expert stockman working throughout northern
Queensland, Western Australia and the Northern Territory.
His experiences were many – the Overland Telegraph line,
the bush race meetings, horsebreaking, then buffalo
shooting and crocodile hunting. Along the way Tom
befriended many people, among them tribal Aborigines,
buffalo shooters and drovers. In his thirties he bought and
sold a number of large stations in the Northern Territory –
Goodparla, Esmerelda, Ingarrabba and Tandidgee.

Tom's autobiography, *Hell West and Crooked*, was
published in 1988 and has since become a bestseller.

Tom Cole died in 1995.

CROCODILES

AND OTHER

CHARACTERS

TOM COLE

SUN
AUSTRALIA

First published 1992 by Pan Macmillan Publishers Australia
This edition published by Pan Macmillan Australia Pty Limited
St Martins Tower, 31 Market Street, Sydney

Reprinted 1994, 1996

Copyright © Gabrielle Cole, Kathryn Cole, Mai Katona 1992

National Library of Australia
cataloguing-in-publication data:
Cole, Tom, 1906-1995.
Crocodiles and other characters.
ISBN 0 7251 0712 X.
1. Cole, Tom, 1906-1995. 2. Country life – Australia – Anecdotes.
3. Frontier and pioneer life – Australia – Anecdotes. I. Title.
994

Typeset in 10/13 pt Aster by Post Typesetters
Printed in Australia by McPherson's Printing Group

With best wishes to my daughter Mai

Mamma, meet Tom from the Territory.

CONTENTS

PREFACE

For almost all of these stories I have drawn on my own experiences. One exception is 'The Man Who Loved Birds' and for this I am indebted to Mrs Kathy Beatty, the wife of the present manager of Terrick Terrick Station. Mrs Beatty went to a considerable amount of trouble to obtain copies of inquest records, contemporary newspaper cuttings and photographs. To Mrs Beatty I wish to convey my sincere thanks.

Of the entire collection the best, in my opinion, is 'Flying Fenton M.D.' His return flight to China in a Gipsy Moth built of wire, wood and fabric was an epic worthy of international recognition. To his charming widow I am grateful for a wealth of information.

I am also indebted to my son-in-law, Laurie Oakes, for considerable assistance and advice on the structure of the two stories, 'The Triangle' and 'Flying Fenton M.D.'. I have always regarded titles as important and Jim Fingleton came up with what I think is an evocative one, 'Crocodiles And Other Characters'. To

David Behrens I am grateful for the photograph that adorns the front cover. A photograph which I thought was long since lost. I also wish to record sincere thanks to my very competent and patient typist Deb Heaata, and to my two daughters, Kathryn and Gabrielle, for unswerving support and encouragement, of which I am in perpetual need.

Several of the stories that appear in this collection have previously been published in Darwin under the title *Spears & Smoke Signals.* It sold out fairly quickly and was never reprinted. I have had so many requests for this modest publication that I have included some of the stories in *Crocodiles and Other Characters.*

Tom Cole
1992

ACKNOWLEDGEMENTS

The publishers would like to thank and acknowledge Collins/Angus & Robertson Publishers for permission to include 'They'll Tell You About Me' by Ian Mudie from *The Blue Crane* © Mrs R. D. Mudi and The Northern Territory Archives Service for their assistance in supplying the following photographs: George Murray, with his family, outside the Arltunga Police Station. NTRS 234, CP 65/1, Bruce Clezy Collection; Constable McColl, starting his last camel patrol in May 1932. NTRS 234, CP 468/1, Bill McKinnon Collection; The Police Station at Barrow Creek. NTRS 234, CP 513/2, Bill McKinnon Collection; The grave of Fred Brooks at Brooks Soak. NTRS 234, CP 500/2, Bill McKinnon Collection; Exhuming Anderson's remains to a casket. NTRS 234, CP 50/12, Stan Cawood Collection; A typical well in the area patrolled by Constable Murray. NTRS 234, CP 51/12, Bill McKinnon Collection; The missing 'Kookaburra' can be seen in the distance as a white object. NTRS 234, CP 50/11, Stan Cawood Collection; The Southern Cross at Alice Springs after returning from Wyndham, 1929. NTRS 234, CP 46/1, Stan Cawood Collection; The 'Kookaburra' as it was found. NTRS 234, CP 51/10, Stan Cawood Collection; Dr Fenton's plane when he landed near the Tennant Creek Post Office to take a sick man to Alice Springs. NTRS 234, CP 64/2, Bruce Clezy Collection.

THE BIG
LIZARDS

'IT'S AGAINST THE law to shoot it and it's against the law to skin it and sell the skin — every bloody thing is protected except us,' he said as he pushed a dead fourteen foot crocodile into deeper water and watched it float away.

That particular saurian had been taking his cattle for years. Only considerable native cunning had enabled it to survive for so long, although the number of scars on its hide testified to some degree of good luck and a greater degree of indifferent marksmanship.

And so the wheels of fortune turn and, as some pundit observed, 'It's an ill wind that doesn't blow some good somewhere'. If only by an act of parliament it wafts on to what was once regarded as an evil and sinister reptile by some, and a valuable source of income by others, transforming it into a treasured tourist attraction.

Most people have read from time to time of

intrepid adventurers dicing with death as they nonchalantly plunge into rivers that are always without exception, 'infested with man-eating crocodiles'. However the death rate of these pioneers was less than minimal. It would be foolish to suggest that there is no danger but it is exaggerated. Cattle are much more susceptible. In the hot weather, in an endeavour to find relief from the heat, they stand in water up to their bellies for hours at a time. Even so the death rate is surprisingly low. Most of the bigger beasts get away, sometimes with frightful wounds that necessitate destroying them.

Man-eaters they certainly are. I was involved with one myself at a place called Marshall Lagoon in New Guinea. According to the records, which were by no means complete, it had taken seventeen people. At the request of the Administration I went to Marshall Lagoon and succeeded in trapping it. Although there were records of individual fatalities, I have never heard of one before or since that approached these figures —

A large crocodile, Northern Territory.

which were well substantiated.

It must be remembered that when a crocodile makes its initial foray into the human area for its food supply and selects Europeans, its life expectancy immediately becomes limited. But this is not necessarily so should its victim happen to be a pagan savage whose superstitions and totems frequently embrace what amounts to a veneration of the crocodile. Following my success in killing the man-eater of Marshall Lagoon, I regretted that I was unable to follow it up with a demonstration of walking on water.

The name alligator is a corruption of El Lagarto, which is Spanish for lizard, while the origin of crocodile is similar but of far greater antiquity. The followers of Herodatus, on seeing these creatures in the Nile, called them Krokodeilos because of their similarity to the lizards of their homeland.

Among the last of the prehistoric animals, twenty-one different species are known to scientists, who believe that they have been around for something like two hundred million years — quite a while. Of these Australia hosts two. One, a harmless fish-eating variety which grows to a length of four or five feet, is known as the Johnstone River, or Johnstonian, crocodile and is essentially a denizen of freshwater streams. The other, a massive brute which, in rare cases, may grow to a length of twenty feet, is known to men of letters as *Crocodylus Porosus*.

Although both are true crocodiles the larger saltwater animal has always been known to bushman of the north as an alligator. This is partly ignorance and partly to differentiate it from its freshwater cousin, the Johnstonian, which was always called a crocodile.

To perpetuate the confusion there are three rivers in the Northern Territory where the saltwater variety has always been plentiful, named the West Alligator, the South Alligator and the East Alligator. From Queensland across to Western Australia there is a liberal sprinkling of Alligator Creeks, an Alligator Lagoon and an Alligator Swamp, but no alligators. The error of nonemclature is understandable.

That delightful American poet Ogden Nash endeavoured to put the record straight in:

THE PURIST

I give you now Professor Twist,
A conscientious scientist
Camped on a tropic riverside,
   One day he missed his blushing bride.
   She had, his guide informed him later,
Been eaten by an alligator,
Professor Twist could not but smile.
'You mean,' he said, 'A crocodile.'

The Johnstone River creature is indigenous to Australia only but, on the other hand, the saltwater animal's habitat extends as far afield as Burma — the widest ranging of them all. Although usually referred to as a saltwater crocodile it is equally at home in fresh water. The female goes well beyond the tidal limits to deposit thirty to forty eggs in its nest, a repository to which it returns year after year. Hidden away in a swamp and composed of leaves and decayed vegetation, the nest is anything up to three feet in height, well above flood levels. The eggs, which are hard shelled, about the size of a goose egg, are covered with a generous layer of composted material which generates enough heat to hatch them.

When the youngsters first see the light of day they scurry to where their mother has been patiently waiting close by and off they go together. They stay with her for some time, at first feeding on her regurgitated food. But life is by no means easy for them. Just about everything eats young crocodiles, including other crocodiles, but they are great survivors. I have frequently shot fully grown specimens that have lost a leg or a portion of their tail, no doubt snapped off by a predatory fish or fellow countryman when the crocodile was small.

A lot of nonsense has been written and much more talked about the size to which crocodiles are supposed to grow — thirty and forty feet being freely mentioned. This I find hard to believe. I first hunted crocodile professionally in 1935 and have shot several thousand. I have been deeply involved in importing and exporting skins in large quantities. I introduced commercial hunting to New Guinea and over a long period of time I have handled in the vicinity of fifty thousand skins. The largest crocodile I have ever shot was on the Victoria River in the Northern Territory — the crocodile measured eighteen feet, nine inches. I shot one in the Kikori Delta of Papua which went eighteen foot six, and another, which lived in the Gogol River until it met me,

A skin from a large crocodile.

was eighteen foot three.

The largest skin I have ever seen was among a shipment which I bought from Borneo. A portion of its tail was missing but I believe that had it been complete it might have made twenty feet. I think it's reasonable to assume that of fifty thousand skins, had any grown much longer than twenty feet, I would have seen at least one. A big crocodile is as easy to shoot as a smaller one, perhaps easier as the target is bigger.

Very little seems to be known of their life span. For the first four or five years they grow at the rate of about a foot a year, progressively slowing down. By the time they reach ten feet they are more than twenty years old. Although they are farmed commercially they are harvested long before they reach maturity, the most valuable skins being eight or nine feet in length.

Most authorities agree that they live to a great age but no one seems to be able to put a time on it. An interesting factor which probably contributes to their longevity is that they renew their teeth, but how frequently I cannot say.

Apart from the size to which some are reported to grow, quite a lot of other nonsense is talked and written about them. There is a widespread belief that their food has to be in a state of putrefaction before they eat it. Although they will certainly eat rotten flesh, their principal diet is fish which they consume as they catch them. It is commonly believed that when they take a human the body is put away in a hole in the bank below the water level, a kind of crocodile larder. This is also a figment of someone's imagination.

Another story that has gained a surprising amount of credence is that their hide will turn a bullet. It should be sufficient to dispel that story by pointing out that when the animal is dead the hide is removed with a knife, a sharp one certainly. Further, I have never heard of a demand for crocodile hides by makers of bulletproof waistcoats.

A creature like a crocodile, because of its nature, its appearance and the kind of place it inhabits, necessarily attracts a lot of glamour, most of which, having been a hunter myself, I regret to say is unwarranted. Nowadays the glamour has lost a lot of sheen. Wear a sheepskin coat by all means, but don't flaunt a crocodile skin handbag even if it has been farmed, which these days is frequently the case.

I first became interested in hunting crocodile commercially while buffalo shooting on the Wildman River in the Northern Territory in 1935. I had been among the buffalo for several years and in that country 'gators, as we mistakenly called them, were plentiful. I had shot a few, usually because of an attack on stock, or because a horse had been mauled, or because I was camped on a waterhole and there was a risk for the lubras when washing or getting camp water.

When an advertisement appeared in a Darwin paper by a Sydney company stating they were buyers of any quantity of crocodile skins, I was immediately interested. An additional source of income was very acceptable — but shooting buffalo was one thing, shooting crocodiles was a horse of an entirely different colour.

However, when it got down to bush lore I had the finest exponents in Australia. My lads were delighted with the prospect. It was a welcome change from the drudgery of skinning buffalo and, as I well knew, crocodile meat was regarded by them as a delicacy. For that reason it had a special appeal. In so many words they said, 'Boss, leave it to us!'

The Wildman River was one of several waterways that ceased to be a confined channel some ten miles before it reached the sea. The Mary and West Alligator were two others that had this feature. In the wet season, which was about four or five months duration, something like seventy inches of rain fell and the rivers flooded out over the huge plains. When the wet ended they drained off into salt arms leaving a lush growth of grasses and a chain of billabongs which were full of crocodiles. Sometimes buffalo were shot close to the banks and for days afterwards it was a common sight to see several crocodiles tearing at the carcases. It was at the head of the Wildman plains where I made my first camp.

The enthusiasm which this new venture generated was quite surprising — my whole team, women included, set to with a will. First they stripped quantities of bark from the paperbark trees that fringed the plains and waterholes. A big tree would yield a sheet anything up to six feet in width and eight or ten feet in length. About two inches thick it is composed of hundreds of layers of tissue-like material and is extremely buoyant. Several sheets, placed one on top of the other, were bound together with vines and dragged into the water. It could carry one man easily.

In the meantime I had been busy too, making harpoons. I was closely watched by Bamboo Charlie who had announced that he was going to be my spearman, a decision which I had no intention of disputing. I fashioned several from a length of half-inch rod which I had cut into sections about a foot long, barbed at the tip — not very elaborate but proved to be effective. The finished product was then lashed to a long rope just above the barb, and fitted into the end of a long pole in such a way that it was tight enough to stay in place but would come away when plunged into a crocodile's back. We were ready.

It was explained to me by old Charlie that we would

start at the first crack of dawn — 'piccaninny daylight'.
It was essential that there was not the slightest breeze

Spearing from a paperbark raft.

to ruffle the surface of the water and the excitement was such on this first morning of our operation that everyone was sitting around the camp fires anxiously waiting for dawn to break.

As soon as there was enough light to see, Bamboo Charlie stepped on to his strange-looking raft, coiled the rope neatly at his feet and, reversing the harpoon shaft, poled his way to the middle. As he floated along he commenced to thrash the water furiously. Very soon a line of bubbles appeared on the surface — something was moving along the muddy bottom. That something was a crocodile! Then the bubbles stopped and Charlie quickly reversed his harpoon and held it poised over the water as his flimsy-looking craft glided over that line of bubbles. Then just as he got to the spot where the bubbles had stopped, he drove the harpoon down into the water with all his strength.

Charlie's thrust had been accurate. There was a mighty swirl as the rope snaked out, more than half of it disappearing immediately. He poled his way to the bank and gave the rope to one of the boys who was waiting excitedly. Willing hands came to his assistance — it was a one-sided tug-of-war.

With a lot of shrieking and yelling from the men, women and children, a ten foot crocodile, thrashing wildly, was dragged to the bank where I quickly despatched it with a bullet to the head. The harpoon, which was firmly embedded in its back, was cut out and Charlie, with a great big smile of satisfaction, poled out into the middle of the billabong again. In a surprisingly short space of time he had harpooned another one, a bit smaller than the first one but nevertheless a useful size.

By ten o'clock a breeze sprang up and ruffled the water to such an extent that the tell-tale bubbles could not be distinguished and so we stopped hunting. We had got five and they were all skinned, salted down and stacked in the shade.

The following day we got four more and Charlie said that we wouldn't get any more from that water-hole so I moved camp to the next one, Alec's Hole, a mile or so further down the plain. We were very successful here, taking fourteen altogether — the smallest being something over seven feet and the largest fifteen. The next water was known as Banyan Point and although no bigger than the last, it yielded a surprising twenty-two. This was the last waterhole on the Wildman. From here to the mangroves, where it was tidal and salt, there was an unbroken plain of several miles.

I intended moving camp over to the West Alligator River where there were two good billabongs in which we knew there were crocodiles. But first I had to have meat. My camp had been living well, mainly on crocodile meat, but I couldn't quite bring myself to eat it, despite the assurances that it was 'number one tucker'. The smell I found quite objectionable, revolting in fact. I must admit that I had been doing very well on duck, geese and barramundi, but I had a yearning to get my teeth into a good steak.

This didn't present any difficulties. I could see buffalo grazing out on the plain a few miles distant so, after getting the camp packing up, I saddled a shooting horse and with a pack horse to carry the meat I rode out just after sunrise. As I approached the buffalo they sighted me and started moving away. I broke into a canter to close the gap and soon they were galloping and I gave my horse his head. He swept across the plain in great sweeping strides, rapidly cutting the distance down.

I was watching the buffalo when suddenly my

mount shied and swerved sharply. It was normal for a
horse to swerve suddenly when galloping across the
plains to avoid a buffalo wallow, a fairly frequent
hazard, but he had shied so violently that I took a quick
look over my shoulder to see what had startled him to
such an extent. To my astonishment, I caught a glimpse
of a fairly big crocodile, obviously dead, lying in the
grass. In few more strides I came to another, and
another. They were all dead. This puzzled me tremend-
ously but I had to put it out of my mind and get on with
the job at hand. I soon caught up with the buffalo and
knocked down a young fat cow.

The pack horse trotted up a few minutes later
driven by one of the camp lads and we took the packbags off to get the butcher's knives out. I asked him if
he had seen the dead crocodiles. 'Ui (yes) boss' he
replied, 'six fella me lookim.' We butchered the cow,
filled the packbags and rode back to the camp. On the
way I did some scouting around. The dead creatures
had aroused my curiosity. I counted eleven altogether.
Turning it over in my mind as I rode along, I formed a
theory which was undoubtedly the answer.

In the first lagoon we hunted we got nine, the next
one, Alec's Hole, fourteen. The last one, Banyan Point,
gave us twenty-two. I hadn't given any thought to the
increased tally as we progressed from one water to the
next, although they were all approximately the same
size. I may have thought that our expertise was improv-
ing, I don't know.

But now there seemed to be a clear answer to the
puzzle. When we started to hunt the first waterhole,
nature's survival instinct went into action. The crocodiles knew that death was abroad and the survivors
moved out during the night. The distances at first were
not so great that they couldn't make it to the next water
during the night's travelling, or at any rate before the

sun got dangerously hot. Of course this accounted for the increased tallies as we went from one waterhole to another.

When we got to Banyan Point there would have been a sharp increase in the crocodile population and I have no doubt that the newcomers would have been able to convey their fear to their reluctant hosts. For reluctant their hosts would undoubtedly have been and this would have contributed to a further migratory move. All mature animals have their own area and they resent intruders. Couple this with our activities and it was easy to understand.

When I started hunting the Banyan Point water another exodus started but this time there was a long way to go. It was several miles across that plain to the safety of the salt arm — it was too far. Creeping along, taking several hours to cover one mile, they would have been killed by the sun before it reached its zenith. A few shady trees would have saved them. I have seen migratory crocodiles lying up under a tree a long way from water, crossing from one water to another.

When I returned to my camp the packing up was completed and we were ready to go. There were no roads of course and travelling across the plain was slow. There were buffalo wallows to be avoided and in places it was very rough due to tracks made wet and then baked hard. Once we got to the other side, the country gave way to timber ridges. A couple of boys had to walk in front to move or cut through fallen timber. By sundown I was at Red Lily Lagoon on the West Alligator River.

By now, having a well-established routine, we were able to swing rapidly into gear. By midday we had a new paperbark raft made but had to wait until nearly sundown for the breeze to die so that the bubbles could be seen. We got only two.

Lying in my swag that night sleep didn't come as quickly as usual. Although it was a hot night and the mosquito net didn't help much, these weren't the reasons for Morpheus being so elusive. Normally, at the end of a day, I could just about sleep on a barbed wire fence. What was occupying my thoughts was all those crocodiles getting away during the night. There were a couple of holes not far away but they were smothered in water lilies — no good to us as the bubbles couldn't be seen.

Red Lily was a big waterhole and I decided that the next day I would put two harpoon men on and clean it out in one fell swoop. I turned over and went to sleep, dreaming of crocodiles slithering past my swag and only a mosquito net between us — which wasn't much protection! I woke up during the night, threw a couple of big logs on the fire and slept a little more soundly.

It was barely 'piccaninny daylight' when I called the camp and in no time they had stripped off a substantial amount of bark and we had another raft floating. There was a lot of competition for the job of harpoon man. After a lot of argument I finally got them quietened down. To the disgust of several others who firmly believed there had been a miscarriage of justice, I appointed a lad who was one of my best buffalo shooters, Shortfoot George, so called because of having lost some of his toes when a baby. He had rolled into a camp fire.

That day was most successful. We took twelve crocodiles, but for another reason it turned out to be one of the most memorable days I ever experienced in my life. Although it frightened five years growth out of me, my entire team, men, women and children with one exception, thought it was the most hilarious thing they had ever seen in their life.

Charlie had just speared a big croc when it took off.

Somehow or other the harpoon rope had got tangled around his ankle and pulled him off his raft with a mighty splash. At that precise moment I was busy sharpening a harpoon. I heard the splash, followed by an almighty shout. I looked up just in time to see Charlie disappear underwater followed by a wake like a battleship. A moment later he surfaced, but very briefly, then he disappeared again.

I grabbed a rifle and ran to the edge of the water. The rest of the camp were running along the bank shrieking with laughter and shouting what sounded like encouragement directed at the crocodile, which was certainly providing them with a magnificent piece of entertainment. They were all splitting their sides. Even old Maudie, Charlie's wife, was laughing as heartily as the rest.

In the meantime the crocodile, effectively harpooned, had got to the end of the lagoon. It stopped for a moment and swam back to a place where there was a steep bank and deep water in an endeavour to find a hiding place. By this time Charlie had freed himself of his entanglement and swam to the bank where I was waiting. I helped him from the water. He was gasping for breath. 'You all right old man?' I asked him. 'Ui, boss' he gasped, 'me orright'. And after he had regained his breath he said 'By Cri boss, me shit plenty!' A statement I had no difficulty in believing.

At the next waterhole I got nine and that wrapped it up for the season.

Only two years later at the end of the hunting season, the 'wet' was approaching and I was settling in at my wet season camp where I had a homestead on the edge of a lagoon, not far from what today is the South Alligator Motor Inn. I was busy paying off my buffalo camp helpers who were even busier preparing for their annual 'walkabout'. This time they were going to Majela Creek where a very important corroboree was to take place over the next few months.

As was normal, they would cross the water not far from my homestead. This entailed quite a lot of preparation. It was a good swim — half a mile I suppose. There would be men, women, children and dogs, all their goods and chattels, rations, spears, didgeridoos. The timing had to be just right too — at the very top tide so that they would not be swept either downstream or up.

Bamboo Charlie, who was one of my foot shooters — and a very good one too — was a very important songman, always in great demand at corroborees like a kind of band leader. His wife Maudie had for many years been my cook. She could make bread in a camp oven with the best. There were ten people to cross altogether, and at least a dozen dogs.

The considerable cargo would be fastened to logs and tied with vines, then pushed across by two or three men. The younger piccaninnies would be tied to a log too. The women would swim behind, assisted by the men in most cases. The dogs trailed along behind. It was quite a procession.

They left my place just before sunrise as they had the tide time worked out pretty well. The racket as they made their way down to the river was indescribable, a mobile Tower of Babel. It was two or three hours later when two panting, breathless boys ran to my verandah. 'Boss, boss! Maudie die finish — big fellow 'gator eatem finish!'

It took a few moments for this to sink in. It seemed like only a few moments ago when they had all trooped away talking, shouting, gesticulating. I didn't have to ask any silly mundane questions like 'Are you sure?' They would be sure all right. I knew there were plenty of crocodiles in the river — big ones too.

They told me that Maudie was swimming to one side of the rest when this huge crocodile swam up to her. It didn't take her in its mouth but clasped her in its forefeet as it swam over the top of her. Then it disappeared in a mighty swirl. It reappeared once and then it had her in its mighty jaws. It dived and it wasn't seen again.

They wanted me to go down to the river straight away and shoot it but there was little hope of seeing it at that stage. But I had to do something, it would have been inhuman not to have done so. Anyway, I had to see the spot so I could make plans to get it, which I knew would not be easy. I sent for a saddle horse and buckled on a cartridge belt as I waited.

The two boys told me the background to the tragedy. I was well aware that to them it was not just a simple matter (maybe 'simple' isn't quite the word) of someone being at the wrong place at the wrong time. There was far more to it than that. It was one of those 'stone country' people, the blacks that lived up in the sandstone tablelands that skirted the coastal swamps and wetlands. The crocodile had been sung and they knew who it was, but something had gone wrong. It was supposed to have eaten Bamboo Charlie. It had made a mistake. Charlie had some enemies up there in the ranges. He was a very important man and his corroborees were powerful stuff. I was told it was some sort of a feud, but it was too complicated for me to follow.

I rode down to the edge of the plain and tied my horse to a tree. I had to walk the rest of the way through mud, long grass and knee-deep water in some places — there had already been some good storms. I floundered my way to the river.

The mangrove fringe wasn't very deep, perhaps twenty yards or so. I looked around for a suitable spot to start the operation, at the same time noting which way the wind was blowing. All the men and women were crying and wailing and had already started cutting themselves with knives, as was customary. I explained to them that there was no chance of us seeing the crocodile that day — something which they knew anyway — and told them what we would do. We all then returned to the station.

I knew that it was going to take some time because the reptile would be gorged on its prey. I told Charlie that he could go out and shoot a couple of pigs. There were plenty around the swamps. He took a rifle and with two or three others strode off into the bush.

They came back with four, two old boars and a couple of youngsters. I took half of one of the weaners. I told the men to take the boars down to the river, let their guts out and hang them up fairly high in the mangroves. We would probably have to wait a couple of days at least before there were any results. In the meantime they all settled down over at their quarters, all thought of the corroboree completely out of their minds. I told them that they must all go down to the river tomorrow, perhaps in the afternoon when the carcases would really start to get high. No matter how gorged he was, that stink would bring the crocodile to the surface.

It was three days before it was sighted. They came running up to the saddle room where I was busy repairing some gear. I immediately grabbed a cartridge belt and rifle, saddled a horse, rode to the edge of the plain and again floundered across to the river where the rest of them were quietly waiting at a spot where they could see the brute surfacing every few moments. I saw it as I quietly waited. It was massive — I reckoned every bit of fourteen feet.

Bamboo Charlie came to me and begged to be

OCTOBER 1935

16 WEDNESDAY 289-76

Ted Sawdy arrived at my camp
this morning to take Dave over
to his alligator camp to run it
for him while he carts my hides
from Spring camp to Kapalga.
I am going to cart all the hides
from Red Rock to Spring with
dray. Decided to start carting
straight away. Will shift camp
to Red Lily crossing tomorrow
& let the boys shoot a few
on N. Alligator. Boat due 26th

17 THURSDAY 290-75

Put 25 hides on the dray
& shifted the camp to the
crossing.
           I instructed boys
to carry on shooting.
              Took one boy & dray
back to Spring camp.
Will cart in the hides
dropped along the road
tomorrow

Entries from Tom Cole's diaries.

allowed to shoot it. I was quite happy to agree. I filled the magazine, handed the rifle to him and got behind to watch the execution. It took some time before he got it in a good position so there would be no mistake. It only took one shot.

I left immediately afterwards. They returned to the station just after sundown. They said that they had found some of Maudie's bones in its stomach and had them wrapped in some paperbark. They offered to show them to me but I couldn't bring myself to look at them. She was a dear old lady and had cooked for me on and off from the first day I shot for George Hunter in 1931.

THE BUFFALO
HUNTERS

IT CAN BE said with a great deal of truth that the herds of wild buffalo roaming the plains and coastal swamps of the Northern Territory owe their existence to the determination of Captain Maurice Barlow, who was appointed the first commandant of Fort Dundas on Melville Island in October 1824.

Named for Sir Phillip Dundas, who was King George IV's First Sea Lord, it is reasonable to reflect on the possible reasons for the choice of this site for a military outpost when the entire northern coastline was available. However, it was not within the province of the new commandant to reason why. He was there and, as October marked the onset of the wet season, he had no time for idle meditation. His concerns would have been: survival for himself, for the detachment of marines, and for forty-four convicts under his command.

He was clearly an officer of ability and resourcefulness. He established and mounted his guns — we are

21

told they consisted of two nine-pounders, four ten-pound carronades and one twelve-pound carronade — and waited for the wet season to take up, aware that he was within the hurricane zone.

When the monsoon swung to the southeast, he despatched the brig *Lady Nelson* to Timor with orders to bring back a cargo of water buffalo. The *Lady Nelson* never returned.

The worthy captain was not unduly dispirited, certainly not sufficiently to abandon his self-imposed task. He next engaged the semi-privateer *Stedcomb*, which was owned by one Captain Barnes, an adventurer of dubious character, whose commission was to deliver fifty buffalo to His Majesty's latest outpost. With foresight, which may have been dictated by the loss of the *Lady Nelson*, Captain Barnes remained ashore. The good ship *Stedcomb* was never seen again, either.

A lesser man could be forgiven for abandoning the undertaking, but the second disaster seems to have strengthened Captain Barlow's resolution. Perhaps like many before and since, he was not deterred by losses borne by His Majesty's government, which was twelve thousand miles away.

The next attempt was more successful, if only marginally so. A French trader in Timor, Monsieur Bechard, agreed to supply fifteen head 'trained to the yoke' and the schooner *Isabella*, perhaps not without a measure of uneasiness, sailed for the Dutch dominion. Two months later she returned, of fifteen buffalos only three survived the voyage.

The Frenchman then contracted to supply two hundred head a year, but the records are shrouded in the mists of time and it is doubtful that he made more than one voyage. It appears that the total number that reached our shores was approximately forty cows and a few bulls. Fort Dundas proved to be a tragic and costly failure and it was abandoned in 1829, but not before the surgeon, Dr Gold, and another man named Green had been speared by natives.

The next experiment was at Raffles Bay on the Coburg Peninsula. The second Commandant, Major Campbell, was transferred lock, stock, barrel and buffalo, or at least some of the latter, to an environment which, to the men anyhow, was no better than the last. This was also relinquished and the next attempt, which was another failure, was at Port Essington.

Port Essington had one brief and fleeting moment of fame, for it was into this outpost that a dying and emaciated Leichhardt staggered after long being given up for dead. Described by a contemporary as 'the most heroic and most hopeless enterprise in the history of the British Empire', the last of the Empire builders sailed away, leaving for posterity a row of graves, a few hundred buffalo and millions of buffalo flies to torment herds of cattle in the coming years. The buffalo which wandered off into the hinterland discovered a perfect environment. They worked their way westward and found coastal plains very much to their liking. Although they were flooded completely in the wet season, from November until about April, there was ample high ground and ridges to which they could retreat. When the plains drained off a lush growth of grasses was uncovered and here they grazed and proliferated undisturbed for the next fifty years.

After four abortive attempts at forming a settlement, one of which included Escape Cliffs at the mouth of the Adelaide River, a town was established at Port Darwin in 1869 and was named Palmerston. By 1870, with a population of forty-three and an Acting Government Resident it was a going concern. Twelve months later it was firmly placed on the map with the commencement of the Overland Telegraph Line, which doubled the population overnight. By the turn of the century, the name of Palmerston had been dropped in favour of the name Port Darwin which was eventually abbreviated to Darwin.

In the meantime, the buffalo which had been abandoned forty odd years previously were doing very nicely. It was fairly well known that large herds ranged across the plains and swamps to the east. A few could be seen in Darwin working in drays for the Chinese who were aware of their capabilities as draught animals. They were regarded as something of a curiosity.

Then a man named Robinson came on the scene and established himself as a customs agent and general trader. Not a great deal seems to be known about him but whenever his name appears he is referred to as E.O. Robinson. Whatever his background was, he had done his homework and he knew that there was a market for buffalo hides. He took a lease of Melville Island where the buffalo had multiplied a thousand fold and came to an arrangement with a young man named Joe Cooper from the southern part of the state.

Cooper was a superb horseman and went to Melville Island and, in his own words, 'shot it out hair hide and tail'. The buffalo were boxed up on the island and couldn't get away, of course, and in five years he shot over six thousand. Those years were not entirely without incident. Over a camp fire and a bottle of rum he told me in graphic detail how he acquired a wife. He had been speared by a Melville Islander in his right shoulder. He managed to break it off but couldn't get it out and he was in a bad way. A young island girl and her mother helped him to a canoe and they started to paddle to Darwin. They were fortunately picked up by a coastal vessel, otherwise it is doubtful if they would have made it in time. When he recovered he married the girl 'bell, book and candle'.

By the turn of the century, professional buffalo hunting was well and truly off the ground. There were well-established markets for the hides, the demand was steady and reliable and for those who gravitated to what was one of the last frontiers of adventure it was a ready-made operation. Quite a few, attracted by the life, found their way down to the coastal plains but not many stayed more than a season as most of them were entirely unsuited to the life and environment. It was a country that soon sorted out the men from the boys. Those who stayed and were successful are still remembered. They were the true professionals who shot year after year, their tallies from a thousand to two thousand bulls in a season of approximately five months, legends in their own lifetime.

Joe Cooper, the Grand Old Man of that fraternity, rightly heads the list. Paddy Cahill of Oenpelli was another together with his equally famous horse St. Lawrence. There was Jim Moles who was killed by a

Tom Cole on his horse Trinket with a wounded bull in the foreground.

buffalo bull at Cannon Hills, Cecil Freer who shot the Point Stuart country, Barney Flynn who was speared on Bamboo Creek and Hazel Gaden who shot over the Marraki country. There was Fred Hardy, who went to the Happy Hunting Ground by way of a fall from a horse and Harry Hardy, his brother of Annaburroo. Their ghosts still ride the plains and the Aboriginals tell stories of them today. I was buffalo hunting for nine years over four to five hundred square miles, on what was known as Kapalga, which ran from South Alligator River to the Wildman River, and, with the exception of Paddy Cahill and Barney Flynn, I knew them all. When Fred Hardy took the fall which broke his neck it was from a horse which he bought from me. As they say, 'it was one of those things'.

The hunters held title over the country which they shot, either a Pastoral Lease or a Grazing Licence. As the buffalo were wild animals, no one had ownership over them. Those who held the country kept fairly well within the limits of their boundaries which were unsurveyed and very haphazard, sometimes established by riding so many miles north, south or what have you, on a horse that walked at about four miles an hour, which gave a very rough guideline.

The hunting season lasted about five months for, although the wet took up around the end of March, the country was not dry or firm enough for hard galloping for some weeks. The long spear grass had to be burnt off too. It grew to a height of ten feet during torrential rains and it wasn't until May that it had fallen over, dried and matted up. It was then burnt and the firing then induced a lush green growth.

Then it was action. The horses, all in great fettle after their wet season spell, were mustered up, shooting horses put on hard feed and shod and Aboriginal helpers, back from several weeks' walkabout, were looking forward to juicy buffalo meat after their bush diet of goannas and yams. Then came the checking of the hundred and one items that went to make up a camp: the saddlery carefully gone over, rifles oiled up and sighted in, ammunition prepared, together with horse shoeing gear, horse feed for the shooting horses, rations, cooking equipment and a substantial supply of salt to cure the hides.

The backbone of a hunter's operation was his horses. An average plant, as it was known, would be about forty or fifty head, of which fifteen or twenty would be in work at a time, and of these his shooting horse was his life's blood. Very few hunters were married as it was not an occupation that lent itself to domesticity. I only ever knew one, but a wife would most certainly rate second in importance to a shooting horse. My first shooting camp was at a place called Gypsy Spring. Good comfortable buildings of bush timber, saplings and bark were quickly run up, although mostly it was a case of renovating last year's camp.

The first few weeks' shooting was on the ridges which were generally heavily timbered and it was hard riding. The plains, completely flooded during the wet, weren't drained off sufficiently for riding until July. At first light, the horses were brought in by the horse tailers and, after a quick breakfast, you swung into the saddle and rode out in the cool morning as the sun was rising. The feel of a powerful horse under you, reefing at the bit, was a time of magic. Trotting along behind were ten or twelve horses for carrying the hides and behind them the skinners trailed along on foot.

Shooting in the timber had one small advantage, if the hunters saw the buffalo first a foot shooter could sometimes get a couple of quick shots in before they galloped away. I always had at least one foot shooter who would walk along in the lead with me. Their eyesight was superb and it was usually one of the boys who spotted the slate-grey beasts first, merged as they generally were in the shade of the forest. The weapon favoured by all horseback shooters was a single shot .303 carbine known as a Martini-Enfield which, although obsolete, was ideally suited for the job. A belt carrying thirty cartridges was generally enough for one day's shooting.

After the first couple of shots, if we were lucky, the buffalo galloped away and then the horseman had to get up on to them as quickly as possible. The horse knew what to do, and the rider's main preoccupation was to watch for low tree limbs. Racing through the timber the horse galloped straight up behind the bull and, just as it got right up to it, swerved while the horseman, carrying the rifle in one hand, fired downward into the buffalo's backbone. It was important for the horse to swerve at the right time, usually with its head level with the beast's flank. If it was too close the

Tom Cole and Ring skinning a buffalo.

falling buffalo could bring down the horse. Without faltering in its stride the horse raced up on to the next, and the next, until they were all shot.

Then the shooter had to ride back and make sure that they were all down. It sometimes happened that the bullet grazed the spine and although it was sufficient to bring it down, unless the spine was broken it would get up and endanger the pack horses and the skinners that soon followed. The buffalo were quickly despatched and then the skinners took over. After the skinning the hides were thrown on to the pack horses, carried bareback and securely fastened with a rope. Back at the camp in the evening, the hides were unloaded close to the water where they were washed, salted down and stacked one on top of the other, each day's shoot being stacked separately.

After a couple of weeks a camp was shot out and the buffalo moved away. As the days went by it meant riding further and further afield until it was time to move on. Most hunters' camps were about ten or fifteen miles apart and so placed that the country was covered. I could shoot the Kapalga country from six camps but later in the year this was sometimes reduced if a waterhole or lagoon dried up — an advantage as it brought the buffalo together.

As the days went by the plains gradually dried out and this was the shooting everyone looked forward to. Covered in couch grass it was good feeding ground and attracted the herds, but it was also good firm galloping in which the shooting horse revelled. It was on the plains that the big tallies were put up. My biggest score in one day was thirty-five bulls and I could have got more but skinning them became a problem. Here the shooting was the easiest part but as the numbers increased the work of skinning and loading the hides on the pack horse became monotonous with the hides heavy in their newly skinned state, weighing up to two hundred pounds.

Day after day the hunting went on and more often than not, the hunters got back into camp after dark. But there were bonuses too. The waters were covered in wildfowl of every description, and there was barramundi in abundance and wild pigs too. One of my camps, Mongulla, was close to a salt arm and here mud crabs were plentiful. There was nothing monotonous about the diet.

Nevertheless, although there may have been monotony at times, there were moments of high drama too. I once got jammed in heavy timber by a wounded bull and although I killed it, it had gored my horse. I immediately dismounted and was horrified to see its intestines hanging out. I had learned over the years that no matter how serious a situation like this appeared there was always a chance. I quickly took halter shanks from the pack horses, joined them together, rigged up a collar rope and dropped the horse to the ground as gently as possible. Even so, more intestines bulged out like a huge bunch of grapes, fortunately not punctured.

Water was quickly carried in hats from a nearby waterhole. In the meantime I was frantically endeavouring to pull thread from a filthy bag in which camp meat was carried. The intestines were cleaned up as far as possible and gradually worked back inside the stomach cavity. With a knife I cut holes in the horse's skin and gradually drew the wound together with the twine. All I could do after that was leave the poor thing and hope for the best. Some weeks later it had completely recovered and of that I was justifiably proud.

In the cool weather in the early mornings before the sun got high the buffalo would thunder along for half a mile or more and it was routine work galloping after them and shooting them. As the weeks went by and the days got hotter they would bail up, and there was always the odd bull that wasn't hit exactly right and would get to its feet — that was trouble.

It is not easy to convey what a good shooting horse meant to the hunter with its intelligence, its courage and stamina, but when faced by a wounded bull of unbelievable ferocity that has to be killed, the rider knew. It was then that he had complete and utter confidence in his mount as an icy calculating coldness took over. Galloping in an arc as the bull charged he could feel the tenseness of the horse under him and drawing it towards him it gradually closed in. Steadying the horse down he led no more than a few feet and leaning back, at exactly the right moment, he fired and killed it. There was no room for mistakes.

At times there were narrow escapes that would enliven the scene. Once, when I was riding through some semi-open country that was broken with clumps of paperbark, fairly dense and perhaps, at the most, a couple of hundred yards through, a couple of bulls jumped up from the shade where they had been lying. Riding Dollar, one of my favourites, I took after them and quickly knocked the first one down while the other, a tremendous animal with horns like sliprails, headed for the protection of the nearest clump of paperbarks which, although extremely dense, had a well-beaten track that I followed. I steadied Dollar down to a canter knowing that when the buffalo got to the other side I would be in open country again and in a few strides would have him.

But that wasn't what happened. Halfway through, on a bend, I suddenly met the buffalo charging back. It all happened so quickly and unexpectedly that there was no time for manoeuvring or even to get a shot away, the timber was too dense. It got its head under my horse's chest, turned it right over on top of me and galloped away. The horse and I scrambled to our feet, I was unhurt but my immediate concern was for the horse which I expected to be badly gored.

To my intense relief it was unmarked. The bull's horns were so wide and the place so restricted that it was unable to do any damage, and it was probably more frightened than enraged. It frightened the hell out of me too — it was as good as a dose of opening medicine. What astonished me was that the beast should suddenly turn and come back — it was dead against the rules. Of course, there was an explanation for it, as I found out. Further along, before the track broke into the open, there had been a heavy fall of timber which was completely impassable. The beast had met with this wall of scrub and turned back.

I think the best shooting horse I ever owned was a bay mare called Trinket — she was certainly the one for which I had the most affection. Standing at only fifteen hands she had a surprising turn of speed and her endurance seemed to be endless. We had some hard rides together. It was from Trinket that I took one of my worst falls and the mare was in no way to blame.

Over the years I had trained several good Aboriginal horseback shooters, one of whom was a lad named Clary. Riding in the lead with me at the head of the pack horse we could handle quite a sizeable mob comfortably. Going through fairly heavy timber one day a single bull jumped up and galloped away. Nodding to Clary I said 'Knock it down', and he galloped after it. A moment later I heard a shot, then another, and another. Obviously he had run into a mob and I immediately took after him at a fast gallop. It was easy enough to follow his tracks and I came to the first bull he had shot. As I did so it jumped to its feet, Trinket had to swerve sharply to avoid it, jump a fallen tree and, with nothing to spare, get between two others. There was no way out of it and I hit one of the trees from my shoulder to my ankle. I was knocked clean out of the saddle and my rifle, of course, went flying.

In a semi-stunned state I was trying to see where my rifle was with one eye and watch the bull with the other. Fortunately it was mortally wounded with the bullet, although missing the backbone, continuing on, probably through its lungs. It gave a last glassy look at me and rolled over. I did the same. After a few moments I got to my feet and found the rifle. It had hit the tree too and the barrel resembled a boomerang. Falls from time to time were inevitable, all part of the day's work, but looking back I sometimes wonder at the survival rate.

Another very good horseman was an Aboriginal whose name was McGinty. He worked for me on and off over the years and he was in Gaden's camp when he got badly horned. I don't recall the details except that his horse fell and a wounded bull attacked him, threw him some distance and McGinty's stomach pierced. One would think it was a case that needed urgent

Aborigines, Clary, Ring and Nim after shooting a buffalo in dense scrub.

medical attention and no doubt it was, but the nearest doctor was a hundred and fifty miles away and to transport the injured man could easily have been fatal so he had to stay where he was. Whatever treatment he got would have been very primitive but with generous assistance from nature he recovered completely after a few weeks.

Brief notes in my diaries record the barest details of a wide range of incidents that are probably the most adventurous in Australia.

JULY 10 1933
Some bush blacks passed through. Said buffalo bull killed Jim Moles at Cannon Hills.

JUNE 2 1934
Word came through from Darwin this afternoon that native boy called Butcher ran amok in Gaden's buffalo camp. He shot and killed Bill Jennings and one lubra. He blew half of Jack Gaden's hand off and wounded another lubra and has gone bush with a .303 rifle and belt of cartridges.

JUNE 5 1934
The lubra that was wounded by Butcher has died — three deaths, now.

OCTOBER 8 1934
There was a fight in the camp last night between Buckley and Joe over a lubra (the eternal triangle). Just got down there in time to take their spears off them and made them fight fists. This resulted in a win for Buckley, he's got three lubras now.

OCTOBER 9 1934
Buckley's two lubras belted hell out of him last

OCTOBER 1935

21 MONDAY 294-71

Went out for beef this morning & got three hides. Nigger swerved into a tree when a bull charged & I got a black shin out of it. Lame in both legs now. Buffalo flies very bad & tormenting horses. Heat almost unbearable, storms working up Would like to knock off, want 180 hides to complete contract Have 620 shot.
Ted ran a few more loads of hides

22 TUESDAY 295-70

Ted & I carting hides. Dray got into Spring camp with one load of hides & left again for Red Rock.
Gave Ring a pack horse & a couple of saddle horses & let him go up to Bamboo creek to try & collect his lubra. Heaviest storm of the season this evening

Entries from Tom Cole's diaries.

night and sent his latest prize bush. Buckley
back to square one (or two?)

JULY 15 1935

Mare Bangle mauled by a crocodile on the
Wildman, badly torn about the head and neck.
Had to shoot her, very upset about this. Set a
trap for crocodile.

JULY 19 1935

Trapped big croc last night.

AUGUST 11 1936

Rode to Bert Coombs' camp to get him to cart
hides to the river opposite my landing. Boat due
soon.

SEPTEMBER 5 1936

Returned to camp and found Paul Bynum from
the other side of the river had come across with
word Bert Coombs died of thirst last week.

SEPTEMBER 27 1936

Found Eagle dead today, one of my best horses,
no obvious reason, in perfect condition.
Probably bitten by a taipan, plenty around,
killed two last week.

JUNE 18 1938

Rode to Turtle Billabong today, found Sam Mini
on my country, in one of my camps, using two
of my horses buffalo shooting. Rectified
situation with light bout of fisticuffs.

SEPTEMBER 3 1939

Left Darwin for Adelaide River. War declared.

I was camped at Harry Gribbon's roadhouse
when I heard on the wireless Prime Minister
Menzies announce: Fellow Australians, it is my
melancholy duty to inform you that we are at
war with Germany. A few weeks later I shot my
last buffalo.

FLIGHT TO
ETERNITY

IN 1928 I was head stockman on Wave Hill, one of Vestey's bigger properties. In 1929 I was managing Bullita, a 2000 square mile cattle station owned by the legendary M.P. Durack.

This was the year the two airmen Keith Anderson and his mechanic Bob Hitchcock were forced down in the desert south of Wave Hill while on a flight searching for Charles Kingsford Smith who had disappeared after leaving Sydney in an attempt to fly to England.

Kingsford Smith had already achieved fame by being the first to fly from America to Australia, and was now a national hero. Having proved that such long distance flights were feasible, he had then planned to fly to England. But after leaving Sydney on the first leg of the flight he disappeared and Anderson and Bob Hitchcock, in an attempt to find him, were forced down in the desert and died of thirst. The results reverberated round the world with a great deal of recrimination and bitterness, finally resulting in a

37

Government Commission of Enquiry.

Charles Kingsford Smith first met Keith Anderson shortly after Charles returned from America where he had been stunt flying for Universal Films. Norman (later Sir Norman) Brearley had started an airline in Western Australia and was the very first to obtain an airmail contract. Kingsford Smith joined West Australian Airways and it was there that he first met Keith Anderson, one of Brearley's pilots. Bob Hitchcock, a highly competent aircraft engineer, was also with the company and the three became friends.

After a spell with WA Airways, Smithy and Anderson left the airline and started a trucking business in Carnarvon, WA, but the itch to fly was all too consuming and they sold the trucking business, making a nice profit on the deal. They then bought two Bristol aeroplanes from their erstwhile employer and formed a company, Interstate Flying Services, engaging mainly in joyriding and barnstorming. Their old friend Bob Hitchcock joined them.

In an endeavour to raise more capital, of which they were painfully short, they advertised for a business partner and it was then that Charles Ulm came on the scene. Ulm was unquestionably a dynamic business man. He had also had some flying experience, but more importantly he had the business acumen and drive that was needed to get the struggling company on its feet.

Unfortunately, with Ulm's arrival, friction started to develop between Anderson, and Ulm and Smithy. Reading between the lines one gets the impression that Anderson was an abrasive character. Perhaps when Ulm came on the scene he felt that he was being edged out. In 1927 Smithy flew round Australia, breaking the existing record by an incredible eleven days. He returned to Sydney amid great rejoicing. On this flight

Kingsford Smith took Ulm as co-pilot, which strained relations with Anderson even further. Shortly after Smithy's record-breaking flight, Keith Anderson, in one of the Bristols, took off with Bob Hitchcock determined to break Smithy's record. He struck vile weather and took four days longer. There were no prizes for coming second. The rift between Anderson and Kingsford Smith was widened.

For some time Kingsford Smith had been obsessed with flying from America to Australia and shortly after Anderson's flight, he and Ulm started to plan the flight, although they were greatly under-capitalised. Nevertheless, Kingsford Smith, always the optimist, was confident that the money could be raised somehow. A couple of weeks after Keith Anderson had completed his flight the three men boarded *SS Tahiti* for the United States. A new and friendly relationship had been re-established.

In San Francisco they carefully examined the merits of various planes, Kingsford Smith finally deciding on a tri-motored Fokker, which would have the endurance and power for a sustained flight. There was a three-engined Fokker owned by the well-known Arctic explorer, Sir Hubert Wilkins, for sale for three thousand pounds and they immediately opened negotiations. Although they were still short of funds, the premier of NSW, Mr Bavin, promised to support them with finance but later reneged. Then, to add to their miseries, they were threatened with legal action. At about this time Anderson became so dispirited that he decided to return to Australia, got on the next boat and left for Sydney.

Then a fairy godfather appeared in the shape of Captain Hancock, a man with extensive shipping interests and a fascination with flying. What followed was an extraordinary sequence of events. Captain Hancock invited Smithy and Ulm to join him for a couple of weeks' cruise off the Californian coast on his private yacht. He was obviously impressed with the two men because at the end of the voyage he offered to finance them from go to whoa. Stunned by their good fortune, they were now able to get the aeroplane out of hock. They christened it the *Southern Cross*. They then set about preparing for the Pacific flight in earnest. The rest, of course, is history.

Kingsford Smith and Ulm landed at Brisbane to an enormous welcoming crowd estimated at three hundred thousand. It was an historic moment. They were feted, wined and dined for the next week. The rewards were immense. They each received the Air Force Cross and the Government presented them with a cheque for five thousand pounds. To cap their moment of glory Captain Hancock presented the *Southern Cross* to them unconditionally. The *Melbourne Herald* opened a public subscription which quickly raised five thousand pounds. In today's money the total of the largesse would probably be in excess of a million dollars.

In the midst of all the celebrations Anderson and Hitchcock each lodged claims for several thousand pounds. It is difficult to see how they could justify claims and the judge seemed to think so too. Both claims were thrown out of court. However, after the smoke of battle had subsided, Smithy and Ulm made a present of a thousand pounds to Keith Anderson. Hitchcock was not included in this extremely generous gesture, or at any rate there is no record of it. With the money Keith Anderson bought a monoplane which he christened *Kookaburra.*

After the successful flight from America to Australia it was Smithy and Ulm's ambition to fly to England in the *Southern Cross* and on March 30th 1929, they took off from Richmond aerodrome in NSW with H. Litchfield as navigator and T. Williams as radio operator, to the resounding cheers of an estimated hundred thousand people.

The intended first leg of the journey was to take them to Wyndham on the north coast of Western Australia but they struck bad weather which not only slowed them down considerably but complicated the navigator's job to such an extent that they missed Wyndham altogether. Shortly before sundown, with the fuel gauges slowly and relentlessly working their way to zero, they realised that they would have to land.

The country they were flying over was hilly, timbered and inhospitable but they came to a reasonably open area. By then there was little or no choice but to land. The country was mainly what is known locally as a claypan, in other words, swampy. This was not detectable from the air and it proved to be a very hazardous landing with the aeroplane nearly turning over as it sank into the soft ground. However, it came to a stop undamaged.

The first thing the men did was examine their resources and, to their horror, found the emergency rations had been cleaned out at Richmond and had not been replaced. All they had was a few sandwiches, some biscuits, five pounds of coffee and a flask of brandy, all of which became their principle means of sustenance. Because of the coffee and the brandy the name of Coffee Royal was bestowed on their forced landing ground.

To the airmen the situation would not have seemed too bad. They had landed unharmed and their aeroplane was unscratched. They only had a very vague idea where they were and, apart from the mission station over which they had passed, they had seen no other sign of habitation. It was really no man's land.

Their greatest handicap was their inability to transmit messages for the power that generated the transmitter was driven by a propeller on a wing. When the aeroplane was stationary and theoretically safe in an aerodrome there was no need for radio communication. The manufacturers didn't anticipate airmen getting lost in places like north-west Australia. Just before they landed they transmitted their last message, 'We are about to make a forced landing in bad country.' Then silence.

When no further messages were sent it was assumed that Kingsford Smith and his crew had crashed. The mission station over which they had passed, Port George, had no means of communication and no idea that the aeroplane was missing. At first their meagre rations were a worry but there was no shortage of water and, as has been frequently demonstrated, a person can live a long time on water. However, they were resourceful men and in a creek nearby they discovered shellfish in abundance. They may not have been up to the standard of the finest rock oysters but would enable them to survive indefinitely.

In the meantime, public agitation was intense. A committee was formed to raise funds for a search and quickly realised a sum of nearly ten thousand pounds, enabling the sponsors to charter aeroplanes. Days went by and there was still no news with aeroplanes searching the country between Alice Springs and across to the Western Australian coast. The Prime Minister, Stanley Bruce, ordered the aircraft carrier *HMAS Albatross*, with half a dozen seaplanes aboard, to take part. Twelve days had gone by when she steamed out of Sydney Harbour.

Meanwhile, Keith Anderson was following events closely and there is no doubt that he was genuinely concerned. He made it known that he would be happy to take part in a search. He was of course familiar with the Western Australian coast from his days with West Australian Airways. A publican with whom he was friendly, John Cantor of the Custom House Hotel in Sydney, agreed to finance Anderson to take part independently. Anderson got in touch with Bob Hitchcock who jumped at the opportunity to accompany him. Their preparations appear to have been hasty to say the least.

In never ceased to amaze me how badly equipped for survival in the bush the early pioneer airmen were in the event of a forced landing. Anderson and Hitchcock were no exception. They flew out of Mascot in Sydney to Richmond, NSW, where they filled up with fuel. *Kookaburra* took off perfectly, although three hundred and ninety pounds overweight. They reached Broken Hill overnight. From Broken Hill they encountered severe dust storms and were blown off course. Their navigation problems, even at that early stage, appear to have been terrifying particularly when considering the type of country they were flying over. Anderson was, even then, concerned about the inaccuracy of the compass. He was flying by guess and by God, two very slender reeds.

From Broken Hill they flew via Blayney to Marree. The next leg of their journey was to Alice Springs and it was on this stretch that severe vibration developed and they landed at Angebuckina. A tappet locknut had become loose. It did not take long to fix and they were soon in the air again. They encountered strong head winds most of the way but managed to reach Alice Springs just before dark on April 9th.

Anderson's anxiety to keep going was evident. He filled up with petrol to full capacity and, after despatching some telegrams, they took off. In those days it was not compulsory for private fliers to submit a flight plan to the Department of Civil Aviation . However, the DCA were deeply concerned, no doubt being fairly well informed of Anderson's difficulties so far. As it was a private flight, they lacked the jurisdiction to enforce any order to stop him.

Anderson was again heavily overloaded by almost a quarter of a ton!! Fuel would have been his principal concern — he would have regarded anything else as an unnecessary handicap. They had the sandwiches, bottles of water and a few tools they had obtained in Alice Springs. No doubt weight would have been uppermost in Keith Anderson's mind and such things as shovels or axes would not have been considered.

It was believed that when he left Alice Springs it was his intention to follow the Overland Telegraph Line as far as Newcastle Waters and then turn north west following the Murranji Stock Route, which would have been clearly visible with bores and waterholes not more than ten or fifteen miles apart at the most. However, when Anderson was about a hundred miles or so, maybe a hundred and fifty miles, out of Alice he inexplicably left the safety of the Overland Telegraph Line and turned north west. He followed the Lander River for a while, but after that there were three hundred miles of the unforgiving Tanami Desert. It was an amazing decision. By taking that course they would not have saved any more than an hour's flying. What makes it even more extraordinary is that Anderson was well aware that his compass was unreliable. The country they were now flying over was completely featureless, nothing but dreary, flat and lightly timbered desert with, what we would call, whip stick scrub.

I would estimate the distance they had flown from Alice Springs to have been about four hundred miles,

The missing Kookaburra *can be seen in the distance as a white object.*

when their old enemy, the tappet, reared its ugly head and started to work loose. It must have been a terrifying situation. Anderson would have realised immediately that, because of the faulty compass, he had only a vague idea where he was. He was anticipating picking up the telegraph line which ran through Halls Creek in Western Australia and there he was in country with which he was familiar from his days with West Australian Airways. An immediate landing was imperative. This he executed brilliantly, the light timber hardly scratching the aeroplane. With the load of fuel that still remained it would have been a hazardous job.

Bob Hitchcock would have been able to fix the loose tappet in a matter of minutes and after this they would have realised their terrible predicament. The country they were in, as I have explained, was very light timber growing in loose sandy soil. Had they even a tomahawk they would have had a chance, but all they had was Keith Anderson's penknife. Sharpening a pencil would have been the limit of its capacity. The four bottles of water would not have lasted them long. Their frantic attempts to clear a runway in that climate would have resulted in heavy perspiration, draining moisture from their bodies which soon they would have been unable to replace. Even with rationing it could not have lasted them two days.

Keith Anderson started to write a diary on the rudder fabric of *Kookaburra*.

> DIARY 10/4/29 to –/4/29. Force landed here 2.55pm 10th April 1929 thru pushrod loosening No2 Cylinder cutting out (as at Angebukina SA on 9/4/29 but temporarily fixed KVA exhaust valve and 25% hp Cleared bit of a runway here which turned out just insufficient or engine coincidentally lost power. Since 12/4/29 all efforts same next to nil, thru having no water to drink except solutions of urines (with oil, petrol, methylate from compass) directed on obtaining sufficient power from engine to permit successful take off. No take off able to be attempted since 11/4/29 due to increased debility from thirst, heat, flies and dust. Left Stuart (Alice Springs) 7.15 local time and followed telegraph line for 100 miles which was intention. Cut off then direct for point between Wave Hill and Ord River Downs. On account cross wind and inaccurate compass and having practically only sun for guidance as map only showed featureless desert determined to above or nor'ard of course which am sure have done. As was in the air 7 hours and am pretty confident had duckpond on my starboard. I figure position now to be…

The tremendous stress Anderson was under shows through in the last few lines of the message. In their

*The Southern Cross at Alice Springs after returning
from Wyndham, 1929.*

anxiety to clear the scrub for a take-off they would
have worked furiously, more so because of their lack
of equipment. They were in a bad way on the 12th
drinking urine and spirit from the compass, which
would have accelerated the pangs of thirst. The next
two or three days would have been a slow and agonis-
ing death.

While Anderson and Hitchcock were slowly dying
of thirst the search for the *Southern Cross* and Kingsford Smith and Ulm was being stepped up. It reached
massive proportions. Then on April 12th Les Holden
(later to die in a crash in New Guinea) found them and
radioed a message that the crew were alive and well
and the aeroplane undamaged.

In the meantime, Keith Anderson's mother and
Hitchcock's wife had been agitating to get someone
interested in the two men who hadn't been heard of
since they left Alice Springs. Unfortunately an argument developed as to who should look for the aeroplane. Eventually the Prime Minister took over and five

Air Force planes were assigned to the search under Flight Lieutenant (Moth) Eaton. The Queensland and Northern Territory Aerial Service (QANTAS) was asked to join in the search and their Chief Pilot, Lester Brain, took off in their very latest aeroplane *Atalanta*.

Captain Brain flew out from Longreach and on to Newcastle Waters Station. From there he headed towards Wave Hill which was to be his base. On the way he spotted the smoke of a bush fire started by the two lost aviators. Soon after he sighted the *Kookaburra* and coming down to within a few feet of the ground he saw the body of a man lying under one wing. He could see only one and although there was no movement he dropped water by parachute. It was April 21st, eleven days after *Kookaburra* left Alice Springs. Captain Brain had no doubt that the man was dead and radioed the news to Wave Hill where there was a wireless station then, flying on to Wave Hill, he confirmed the grave news.

Vestey's Chief Pastoral Inspector, Alec Moray, was at Wave Hill and immediately took charge of the ground party. Cattle Creek, a tributary of the Camfield River, was the last water. It was a small watercourse and at that time of the year, a couple of months after the wet season, would have long stopped running, but there was sufficient water for a base from where the ground party could strike out into the desert. I would think that from there to the stricken aeroplane and the dead airmen would be about sixty miles. Flight Lt. Eaton joined the ground party. It took two days to reach the *Kookaburra*. The dead man lying under the wing proved to be Bob Hitchcock, Keith Anderson's body was found about a mile away. Both men were buried where they lay.

Up to that time, and following the finding of the *Southern Cross* and Kingsford Smith and his compan-

Exhuming Anderson's remains to a casket.

ions alive and well, the newspapers had been pouring out panegyrics of joy at the successful end to the search — until a well-known scandal sheet, *Smith's Weekly*, came out with its front page blazing on April 27th:

QUESTIONS TO BE ANSWERED
THE SACRIFICE
SOUTHERN CROSS FIASCO

The headlines were followed by a series of questions implying that the whole thing was a put-up job engineered by Smithy to obtain publicity. There was a full front page of rabid journalism. *Smith's Weekly* intended to wring the story dry. Once it started there was no stopping. The rest of the newspapers in full throttle took up the story, adding fuel to the flames.

Kingsford Smith was pilloried. It was an example of fickle public opinion. Overnight he became a calculating villain who had caused the death of two mates. The ensuing publicity was of such a sensational nature and the pressure so great that the Prime Minister, Mr Stanley Bruce, opened an enquiry. It always seemed to me that the whole affair generated by the press was some form of journalistic insanity.

No matter how you looked at it, it was difficult to see Kingsford Smith's landing as a calculated stunt. They had flown through vile weather, lost their bearings and, when their fuel tanks were almost empty, landed on a flat that no pilot in his right senses would have attempted had he not been compelled to do so. There was no way it could be construed as anything but a forced landing. That the plane survived without damage and after being filled up with fuel and flown out was something in the nature of a miracle. Smithy and his crew were completely exonerated from any suggestion that this was a publicity stunt.

Shortly after the enquiry was completed Smithy, Ulm and their crew made a fresh start on their planned flight to England and predictably broke the record, again by a considerable margin. The 'Coffee Royal' affair, however, had left a nasty smell from which Kingsford Smith never recovered.

Anderson and Hitchcock became posthumous national heroes. The salvaging of the *Kookaburra* was widely discussed but because of the expense involved nothing came of it. Charlie Berg, whom I knew quite well and who maintained the bores along the stock route and was involved in exhuming the bodies and bringing them back, offered to buy the aeroplane but nothing came of that either.

Gradually it was forgotten until recently when Dick Smith became interested and, at tremendous expense, initiated and took part in a search and found the *Kookaburra*. Finding it was a remarkable feat. It had lain there for fifty years, ravaged by bush fires and there was little left of the once proud aeroplane. It was

The Kookaburra *as it was found.*

Dick Smith's intention to restore it which would have been at considerable expense to himself. Unfortunately the Northern Territory authorities stepped in, rejected his offer and claimed the wreck. It was trucked to Alice Springs where it is, I believe, on display. It is extremely doubtful that it will ever be restored.

Of the various players in the drama I knew quite a few — Alec Moray of course, all the Aboriginals who were engaged in the recovery of the bodies of Anderson and Hitchcock were from the stock camp of which I was head stockman. Some years later I met Flight Lt. (Moth) Eaton in Darwin. By then he was a Wing Commander and I recall promising to get him a set of buffalo horns but I am fairly sure he never got them. I probably promised more buffalo horns than I ever shot buffalo — and that's an awful lot.

Sir Charles Kingsford Smith, who was knighted following his successful flight to England, had a brother, Eric, who was one of the founding officers of the Royal Australian Navy. I met Eric, who was known to his friends as Wilfred, in New Guinea in 1968 when he was on a visit to his son who, like myself, was a coffee planter in the Western Highlands. I got to know Wilfred very well and he talked at length of his famous brother, for whom he obviously had a great and sincere admiration.

He believed that his brother was shabbily treated by the Commonwealth Government for although his company, Australian National Airways, made numerous competitive bids for airmail contracts he was never successful. Wilfred always believed that it was because of the 'Coffee Royal' affair. He thought that the Government regarded the finding as a sort of 'Not guilty but don't do it again' verdict.

During our friendship Wilfred frequently expressed a wish to visit the Sepik River, about which he had heard so much and, knowing that I had had a great deal of experience on the river during my crocodile hunting days, he asked me about it. I was able to give him a letter of introduction to a friend of mine, Madsen, who had handled the Sepik River for me, buying skins from native hunters.

Wilfred arrived at Angoram, a small township on the river where Madsen was running a sawmill and about to take delivery of an aeroplane, a Beechcraft Musketeer, a low-wing, single-engine monoplane. The aircraft was delivered to Madsen by a de Havilland test pilot named Ignatroff, an ex-Fleet Air Arm pilot of considerable experience. Having familiarised Madsen with the aircraft, the de Havilland pilot planned to return to Sydney and Madsen suggested that he fly him to Port Moresby from where he intended to catch the southern plane to Sydney.

It was July 1968 when they took off from Angoram, the de Havilland pilot, Madsen and his wife and Wilfred Kingsford Smith, who took the opportunity to return to the Highlands and his son's plantation. They flew out

18 MONDAY 18-348

Ordered rations and packs up

19 TUESDAY 19-347

Saw Kingsford Smith ~~arrive~~ arrive from England with mail Left Darwin and camped Rapid Creek

20 WEDNESDAY 20-346

Left Rapid Creek and camped Mee Wah Lagoon where Herberts are repairing yard

Entries from Tom Cole's diaries.

of Angoram on the first leg of the journey, to Kagam-uga, which was the airstrip for the little Highland town of Mt Hagen and was of international standards. It was a departure point for travellers to Indonesia, Hong Kong, Singapore etc.

The following morning the party were out at the airport at first light on a beautiful clear morning. When they took off it is believed that Ignatroff was at the controls and he selected a cross strip in preference to the main runway. The aeroplane appeared to have taken off comfortably after a short run. When it was only a few hundred feet from the ground it took a sudden nose dive, burying itself in the ground at the end of the runway and killing all on board instantly.

It was an inexplicable accident and, as far as I can recall, no logical reason was given for it. The aeroplane was in perfect condition. Bob Gibbes, who operated Gibbes Sepik Airways at the time and who had had considerable experience flying in and out of Kagam-uga, told me that using the cross strip at times one could strike, as he expressed it, 'a dirty downdraught'. Surrounded as it was with towering mountains, Mt Hagen itself rising seven thousand feet above the valley floor, this could be a reasonable explanation.

I suppose it is ironical that Sir Charles Kingsford Smith's brother, a naval man, should be killed in an aircraft accident.

GUNS OF
SHAME

IN 1928 CONISTON Station was one of the most isolated cattle properties in Australia. It lay about one hundred and fifty miles north-west of Alice Springs and was owned by Randal Stafford, who had originally selected the holding when it was crown land.

Prior to taking up the Coniston country, Stafford had been a telegraphist at Barrow Creek Telegraph Station. Although a competent bushman with sound knowledge of cattle, he was quite different to the average run-of-the-mill cattleman at that time — when survival in the harsh environment of the outback depended on an unusual degree of toughness. In many respects he was a gentle man and I believe this characteristic contributed largely, if not entirely, to his survival from a series of events that are among the most dramatic in Australian pioneering history.

Coniston Station was not an unusually big area by the standards of those days — it was slightly less than one thousand square miles. It included some desert country but also well-grassed plains and river flats, carrying feed that produced sleek, fat bullocks, which always commanded good prices.

But water was a perennial problem. The Lander River ran diagonally through the middle of Coniston and was fed by Warburton Creek and one or two others of a lesser nature. There were springs that yielded clear, cool water but they varied considerably in the volume they produced. After the wet season when they had been replenished by the rains, the springs would run for a short distance, but some were of such miniscule nature that as the dry season progressed they would gradually subside back to the sandy earth, leaving a damp patch. They were so insignificant that they didn't even rate the name of 'spring' but were referred to as 'soaks'.

Aborigines at Alec's Hole on the Wildman Plains,
Northern Territory.

The Aboriginals of this area, the great survivors of the unforgiving desert in the centre of Australia, drew on the life-giving water of the soaks long after they had receded below the surface. With yam sticks and boomerangs, they would scrape away the wet sand until they reached water, which was usually only a few feet below the surface. They would bail it out using coolamons — wooden dishes that they had with crude tools laboriously fashioned from gum trees and such like.

This was a sparsely settled country, the settlement being governed by the availability of water. North of Coniston there was nothing but desert for five hundred miles, to the west maybe one thousand. There are blue patches on the maps of this area that cartographers use to indicate 'lakes' — some of them, like Lake Mackay, are one hundred miles across — but a closer examination will reveal in brackets the word 'salt'. From Coniston it is another one thousand miles to the sea and there is very little in between.

Randal Stafford's closest neighbour was Nugget Morton, who owned Broadmeadow Station. Broadmeadow does not exist under that name today, it is most probably what is known as Mt Barklay Station, which is one thousand square miles, through the middle of which the Lander River also runs. Nugget Morton was built like one of his own bulls and looked twice as strong.

Then there was George Murray, one of the most competent Northern Territory mounted police, who had about fifty thousand square miles of country to keep in order, an area which is about half the size of Europe. There was a government resident named Cawood, a sort of administrator, second class — who lived in Alice Springs and did what Canberra told him to do.

George Murray, with his family, outside the Arltunga Police Station.

Then there was an Aboriginal named Bullfrog, who had been given this name by a white man when he was a piccaninny because of his distended belly and the funny noises he made. Bullfrog, when he grew up, became an important tribal leader and, like a lot of Aboriginal tribal leaders, did plenty of talking and gave a lot of orders to others.

Bullfrog decided that all the white men in his country would have to be killed because they had taken their country without asking, commandeered the precious water, wanted their women for a few sticks of tobacco and also had a lot of flour, tea and sugar locked up in their stores.

The other party in this story was one Fred Brooks, a man who was to give his name to one of the obscure soaks under circumstances that certainly were not his choosing. Freddy Brooks had two camels and at the time of this story he was about to start off from Coniston Station. He had stocked up with rations that Randal Stafford had brought out from Alice Springs in his old beaten-up truck. Stafford asked Brooks what he was going to do, where he was going, and he said that he would probably wander down the Lander and do some dog stiffening. 'Dog stiffening' was an expression used by bushmen who trapped or poisoned dingoes. In the Territory dingoes were always referred to as 'dogs', which they are of course. Stafford told him to be careful, which was not merely a figure of speech; there was a good deal of uneasiness among the white settlers and others, including the miners and prospectors too.

Bullfrog had been talking about what he was going to do. He was going to kill all the white men or, at any rate, his tribe was going to kill everyone. Nugget Morton was to be killed first — Bullfrog was personally going to do this because he had suffered at Nugget's powerful hands.

But as it turned out, Nugget wasn't the first man to be killed. Freddy Brooks was. Brooks left Coniston with two young Aboriginal boys who looked after his camels. They watered them, took them out to where there was feed, hobbled them, and brought them back in the morning. Their names were Skipper and Dodger. Skipper was about fifteen and Dodger was perhaps a year younger.

Brooks had wandered down the Lander River and found his way to a small soak where there were some blacks camped, maybe ten or fifteen. There wasn't much of a water supply, but enough. The blacks had cleaned it out and made a pool which, if lowered, quickly replenished itself.

It was the early morning of August 7th and the two lads left just as the sun was rising to bring the camels in to water. Brooks intended to stay for a day or so. He had been fairly successful with his 'dog stiffening' having already got several scalps for which he could

collect the bounty of five shillings each. He had dug
some rabbit warrens out for the rabbits which he used
for bait. To get them he had to dig very deep, so the
warrens were substantially enlarged. He didn't know it
but he was digging his own grave.

More blacks had arrived at the soak the previous
night and among them was Bullfrog and his wife,
Marangali. Bullfrog went to Brook's camp with some
dog scalps which he would trade — Marangali was
with him. Brooks asked Bullfrog if his woman could
wash some clothes for him, to which he agreed. After
Marangali washed the clothes it was sundown. She
stayed and later, after it got dark, she joined Brooks in
his bed. The trouble was Brooks had not given Bullfrog
the rations that he had promised — the payment to be
made for the use of his wife after 'the goods were
delivered'. There was nothing unusual about this but it
may have been the opportunity for which Bullfrog's
people, the Walbiris, had been waiting.

There does not seem to be any doubt that a massacre had been planned but not very well planned. Harry
Tilmouth who was part-owner of Napperby Station
was threatened by a group of Walbiris who were
armed with boomerangs and spears. They started to
surround him but he fired his rifle and killed one. This
discouraged the rest for some time but it was merely a
postponement.

On the morning of August 7th, just as dawn was
breaking, Brook's two lads walked out to bring in the
camels. It was a precautionary measure because if
they were not brought to the camp daily they were
likely to stray a little further each day. Also when
camels are used to getting water every day, or at least
every second day in the cooler weather, they need it. To
go for long periods like a week, they have to be trained
and kept from water for two days, and then three and

four and so on.

That fateful morning, Fred Brooks left his swag, perhaps not quite so rested as he would have been had he not had company. No doubt his sleep was broken and it was then that Bullfrog killed him. At close range a boomerang is an effective and terrible weapon and blood gushed from Brooks' throat where Bullfrog's weapon had struck him. Although he was mortally wounded, Marangali leapt behind him and pinioned his arms as others joined in slashing at the white man with some knives and tomahawks. He was quickly hacked to pieces. Brooks' remains were then stuffed into the enlarged rabbit burrow which he had delved into the day before. But they couldn't get all the body in and one leg was left sticking skywards. They then ransacked his camp.

Then the two young lads arrived with the camels. They were only children and when they learnt what had happened to 'old Fred' they were shocked and fearful. Dodger and Skipper were not of the Walbiri clan and could possibly join their erstwhile boss. They were in a state of mortal terror.

Bullfrog, still holding a bloodstained boomerang, told them what they had to do. They were to take the camels, return to Coniston and tell Randal Stafford that old Fred had got sick and wandered off into the bush during the night and had probably died. They thought they had better come back to the station and tell someone. When Dodger and Skipper reached Coniston, to their relief Stafford was not there. He had gone to Alice Springs and no one was sure when he would be back. Bullfrog had told the boys that if they told anyone what had happened, that Brooks had been murdered, then he would find them no matter where they hid and would kill them. But it was a secret that was far too great to keep and, although they whispered it in the still and silent watches of the night, it spread like bush fire, from camp to camp, from station to station. It was still a 'secret' and no one must know! No one was to tell anyone!

Randal Stafford returned to Coniston and was told immediately. It was a tremendous shock for he had a soft spot for the old trapper. They had been mates for years and, although Stafford shared the general uneasiness which prevailed regarding the blacks, now something had happened that seemed unreal — unreal because of it taking place on his very doorstep. When situations like this arise it is mostly unexpected because people are inclined to believe that 'it can't happen to me'.

Mounted Constable George Murray was stationed at Barrow Creek and Stafford quickly got word to him. He too was shocked as Fred Brooks was the last man he would have expected to be killed by blacks. He was of a kindly disposition, everyone liked him and he would not have had an enemy in the world. It was well known that the blacks liked him too. The general

The Police Station at Barrow Creek.

reaction was, 'not Fred Brooks!' If it had been anyone else I believe that the reaction may not have been of such a shocked nature.

Murray's first action was to get in touch with Cawood, the Government Resident and ask for some support. He spoke to him on the Overland Telegraph line telephone from the Barrow Creek Telegraph Station. Cawood's first reaction to the news was, 'I knew it would bloody well happen, I knew it!' He went on to tell Murray that he would have to handle it himself. He had no one to send him and he told him to get whatever help he could from the stations.

Murray spelt it out. 'Have I got a free hand?' he asked. 'Yes,' said Cawood. 'You've got a free hand.' Those words set the stage for one of the most shocking massacres in Australian history.

Murray had one tracker, Paddy, twenty or thirty police horses and all the necessary equipment, a Colt revolver, a .44 calibre Winchester rifle and plenty of ammunition. He rode to Coniston and told Stafford that he wanted as much assistance as he could give him. He told him too that Cawood had given him a free hand. Stafford had a well-sinker named Jack Saxby who was working about twenty miles from the station. He was quickly brought in together with Billy Briscoe, another of his men who arrived the next day. With Stafford, Saxby and Briscoe, Murray had three white men. He also had Paddy, his tracker, and one of Randal's black stockmen, Major, who was an exceptional tracker and a half-caste named Alec Wilson.

While the expedition was preparing to leave the Coniston homestead, two Myall bush blacks arrived and on seeing the police patrol turned to run. Tracker Paddy was too quick and managed to grab one. Stafford's Major attempted to hold another but he broke away. Hearing the commotion Murray came running over to their assistance. The black who had broken away had managed to get hold of a neck chain with which Paddy intended securing them and he faced Murray slashing at him. Murray drew his revolver, fired and dropped him. Although he was bleeding freely from the head, he was not dead and he and his companion were both secured.

In the meantime, the blacks who had been at the soak where Brooks was killed were not unduly perturbed by the murder and had all moved to another waterhole only a few miles away. They must have been very confident that there was not going to be any immediate repercussions anyway. If so, it was a confidence that was about to be rudely shattered.

Mounted Constable George Murray reached the soak which now had become 'Brooks' Soak'. He inspected the remains of the kindly, harmless bushman, and the awful stench, the swarms of flies and ants, the leg sticking out obscenely from the warren deeply affected him.

'The bloody bastards,' he said. 'The bloody murdering bastards, they'll pay for this.' What the blacks called, 'Time belong killem allabout' was about to begin.

After burying Fred Brooks, Murray's trackers quickly got on the trail of the blacks who had been camped at 'Brooks' Soak' and it was with some surprise that they were discovered only a few miles away. When the news was received, Murray gave clear instructions that there was to be no shooting unless attacked and no women or children were to be harmed. But whatever his intentions may have been it didn't work out that way. When the police party appeared at the camp the blacks began to hurtle their spears and boomerangs, none reaching their mark.

Murray got to the camp first and was soon locked in a hand-to-hand struggle with some Aboriginals when Briscoe and Wilson arrived. Suddenly they were all shooting. All that is except Randal Stafford who trotted up when it was all over. There were several dead, including one woman who was identified as Marangali, Bullfrog's woman, who had held Brooks when he was killed. Of Bullfrog there was no trace.

The following morning Stafford asked Murray

The grave of Fred Brooks at Brooks Soak.

what he was going to do next. 'I'm going to get Bull-frog', was the grim reply. Stafford was shocked by the shooting and was anxious to get away. He told the constable that he would like to leave the party as he had a lot of branding to do. This was probably right, there is no busier month in a cattleman's calendar than August. Murray would have realised that Stafford had no stomach for this sort of thing, whereas Briscoe and Saxby seemed to be enjoying it. Stafford rode back to his homestead.

Murray pressed on going from one blacks' camp to another and always there was shooting. They could not find Bullfrog and Murray wanted him more than anything else. They rode for two weeks and, after some more shooting, they returned to Coniston with two prisoners.

From Coniston he went back to Barrow Creek where he prepared his report for the Government Resident. It was fairly brief and to the point. The constable had ridden nearly a thousand miles under difficult conditions and had been attacked a number of times. The party had shot seventeen blacks in self-defence and had taken two prisoners. Cawood congratulated him and told him he had done a good job. But it was only the beginning.

Another fifty miles down the Lander River was Nugget Morton's homestead. It was the end of August and he was not at home. Like nearly every cattleman, he was busy. It so happened that he was at Boomerang Waterhole. He had ridden there on his own, which was unusual, to have a look at the water and perhaps 'show the flag'. He was not very happy to find twenty or thirty blacks camped there. Not only did they represent a disturbing element to the stock watering there but Morton had no doubt that they intended spearing cattle, if they had not already done so. But there was more to their presence than that. They intended killing Morton.

Bullfrog had said that Morton must die and he himself intended to take a prominent part in the killing. But just then he had prudently taken himself off. Nugget had dismounted, lit a fire and put a billy on. His pack horse and saddle horse fed around. He loosened his belt and laid it over a log. It carried a revolver and was consequently heavy.

He was seated on the log when he was attacked, first by four Aboriginals who foolishly thought that they were equal to this man. It took very little time for them to find out that they had made a serious miscalculation. Four more came to their aid and now the donnybrook was reaching alarming proportions. Eight men were not enough to subdue this bull of a man. His strength was unbelievable and he knew how to use it to the best advantage for he had been a professional wrestler. More Walbiris joined in and this may have saved him because there were so many of them they were getting in one another's way. Some were losing enthusiasm too — it was no fun being hit by Nugget Morton.

Badly battered, Nugget knew that unless he could get to his revolver he was lost. He had to get hold of it somehow. He was streaming blood and almost blinded when his hand closed on that precious weapon. He had a broken thumb where he had been struck by a nulla-nulla but that wasn't going to affect his aim. He fired one shot at his closest assailant. The man's head exploded as the bullet went in one side and came out the other. As one, the others turned and ran. This man was not human, he was a devil incarnate. They were right about that too.

Although Nugget Morton survived he was in a bad way. He had to ride twenty miles back to his homestead. Two days later he rode into Ti Tree Well where he was attended by an Australian Inland Mission nurse, who stitched up frightful scalp wounds and extracted pieces of boomerang and nulla-nulla from his head. She reported the atrocity to Sergeant Noblet, Murray's superior officer, at Barrow Creek. She did not have to embellish the story to make it sound horrifying.

By this time Constable Murray had built up a considerable measure of fame as a man who could fix the murdering blacks, which he himself did nothing to diminish, he was a natural for the job. Once again he was bouncing his way over a track that was becoming familiar to him. Two trackers brought his horses along. He passed through Coniston and went to Broadmeadow where Morton was waiting for him. Morton's wounds were healed, except for those to his self-esteem. He badly wanted revenge.

It was close to the end of September when the two men rode away from Broadmeadow Station and it was three weeks later when they returned. Murray's second foray was not to apprehend murderers, but to investigate the attack on Morton. The whole story has never been told but, at any rate, the 'investigation' appears to have started at Tomahawk, a waterhole down the Lander where at least four Aboriginals were shot. At Circle Well two more died — and not from

A typical well in the area patrolled by Constable Murray.

natural causes. They went to a place called Tippenba which was never mentioned in any enquiry but it is certain that many more were shot there. At Dingo Hole it is believed twenty may have been shot, including women and children. It was October when the two men returned to Morton's place. It may have been because they ran out of ammunition, or, on the other hand, they may well have run out of blacks. In any case, Murray had to get to Darwin with the two prisoners who were charged with the killing of Brooks.

The trial of the two Walbiris for Brooks' murder was by no means a simple straightforward affair. It was presided over by Mr Justice Mallam, who was not renowned for his equanimity, and his difficulties were compounded by some of the jurymen who got drunk during a lunch break. This necessitated a new jury and, of course, a new trial. The same witnesses took the stand again but this time their evidence was quite different to what they had given the first time.

Murray took the stand and he did not come out of it very well at all. Just before the conclusion of his examination, the Judge asked him if it were necessary to shoot to kill in every case. In his reply Murray said, 'Yes, I shot to kill, what was the use of a wounded blackfellow to me a hundred miles from civilisation?' That must surely go down in history as the most remarkable excuse ever put forward to justify shooting innocent people.

In the meantime, the last series of shootings which Murray and Morton had engaged in was gradually becoming known. Even with official support and connivance it is difficult to keep quiet the killing of fifty or sixty people. There was an extremely tenacious lay preacher named Athol McGregor who had heard some disturbing reports of Murray's activities, particularly the expedition with Morton. He was determined to find out more. He soon discovered that smoke screens were not so difficult to penetrate after all. There were now a lot of people who were deeply disturbed at such indiscriminate killings over an area as wide as seventy to eighty miles. Reasonable people, even those who were not exactly 'pro blackfellow', were finding the rumours difficult to stomach.

Reports were not only appearing in the southern Australian papers but in such prestigious overseas journals as *The Times* of London and *The Manchester Guardian*. Reports even penetrated the walls of the League of Nations. The pressure became so great that the Prime Minister, Stanley Bruce, agreed to an enquiry. A police magistrate named O'Kelly was appointed and it opened in December 1928 and, except for a brief Christmas break, continued through to the end of January.

Depending on whose side you took, and there was more than one side, it could be described as a success or a failure. The Board found that in all cases the shooting was justified! The most ironic feature of the whole thing was that Bullfrog, who started the killing, escaped entirely.

THE MAN WHO
LOVED BIRDS

Me, I'm the man that dug the Murray for Sturt to sail
    down,
I am the one that rode beside the man from Snowy
    River,
and I'm Ned Kelly's surviving brother (or did I marry
    his sister?
I forget which), and it was my thumbnail that wrote
    that Clancy
had gone a-droving, and when wood was scarce I set
    the grass on fire
and ran with it three miles to boil my billy, only to
    find
I'd left the tea and sugar back with my tucker-bag,
and it was me, and only me, that shot through with
    the padre's daughter,
shot through with her on the original Bondi tram.
But it's a lie that I died hanging from a parrot's nest
with my arm in the hollow limb when my horse
    moved from under me;

71

I never die, I'm like the Leichhardt survivor I
        discovered
fifty years after the party disappeared; I never die,
                        They'll Tell You About Me, Ian Mudie

MANY YEARS AGO I was buffalo hunting on the Wildman
River in Arnhem Land. My cook at that time was a
grand old bushman by the name of Dave Cameron.
Dave was one of those itinerant bush workers who had
done just about everything: shearing, fencing, well-
sinking and finally, like many of his kin, camp cooking.

Dave was a great raconteur and of all the many
stories he told me over the years of our association
there was one of such a macabre nature that I have
never forgotten it. It happened on a sheep station called
Terrick Terrick, which is in the Blackall district of
Queensland. Since Dave told me the story I have heard
it repeated quite a few times round that great bushman's forum, the camp fire, and always there were
some variations and the variations were extremely
wide, to the extent of some declaring that it was
entirely fictitious.

In an endeavour to find out what really happened, I
wrote a letter to the *Stockman's Hall of Fame* newspaper. I was rewarded with an almost immediate reply
from Mrs Cathy Beatty, the wife of Mr Rob Beatty, who
is the present manager of Terrick Terrick Station.

Terrick Terrick Station was first started up in 1864
by two adventurous Victorians, John Govett and
James Thompson. They must have been extremely
adventurous to have gone so far afield in those early
years. Australia had only been colonised 76 years. It
was only two years earlier that the continent had been
crossed from south to north by John McDouall Stuart,
and it was six years before the Overland Telegraph had
even started in 1870.

Initially stocked with sheep, Terrick Terrick ran the normal gamut of drought and flood and, after changing owners from time to time, it came into the hands of an English investor, one Charles Rome. It is doubtful if Rome ever laid eyes on the place, which in those days was by no means unusual. Rome sold Terrick Terrick to a wealthy Victorian, Donald Wallace, who apart from having extensive pastoral interests was prominently associated with bloodstock.

Wallace's principle claim to fame was that he owned the mighty Carbine, unquestionably the best horse in the world at that time, and possibly any other. After winning thirty-three races from forty-three starts and thirty-three thousand pounds in prize-money, Wallace sold this gallant horse to the Duke of Portland for thirteen thousand guineas.

Some time after buying Terrick Terrick, in the early 1880s, Wallace met Richard Gardiner Casey (who was the father of one of Australia's more prominent governors general). Casey was thirty-seven years of age and had already established himself as an astute and experienced businessman in pastoral and associated matters. Wallace, clearly impressed with Casey, offered the younger man a managing partnership in Terrick Terrick.

Casey took up the management with enthusiasm but it turned out to be a turbulent and unhappy association. The property was saddled with horrendous debts, being in the hands of a London financier, to the extent of two hundred thousand pounds, which was a massive sum in those days. After ten years the partnership was dissolved and some years later the property was taken over by a company with the ominous name of The Australian Estates & Mortgage Company.

In 1912 The Australian Estates & Mortgage Company were embarking on an extensive improvement programme. As the lack of water was a perennial problem they employed a well driller. Drilling for water is not a very complicated business, but in those days of course it involved a lot of hard slogging. There is no natural flow of water at a well site, however, water, together with firewood, is used in vast quantities to feed the insatiable demands made by the steam engine that drives the drilling machinery.

Tom Walsh and an offsider operated the drilling machine, and Alf Devaney was the team driver and it was his job to keep up the supplies of wood and water. For this purpose he had a wagon and a team of seven or eight horses. There would be a couple of one hundred gallon tanks on the wagon, a gallon of water weighs ten pounds, so two hundred gallons would be a fair load for seven or eight horses. So, with carting loads of firewood and water and seeing that his horses were looked after, Devaney would have had a seven-day week job.

One morning while out mustering his horses for the day's work, Devaney saw a galah fly out from a hole in a gum tree. Riding closer, he could hear young birds twittering. The next day, October 21st, without saying where he was going, he took a quiet horse and rode out to the tree where he had heard the young birds. His black and white dog followed him.

When he got to the place where he had heard the young birds chirping he manoeuvred his horse along-side the tree, stood up on the saddle, and put his arm in the hole to retrieve the nestlings. It would seem that the distance down to where the nest lay was much further than he had anticipated and his arm was down in the hollow to the elbow. Even then he may not have been able to reach them. Perhaps in his anxiety to do so his feet, encased as they were in riding boots, slipped from the saddle, or perhaps his horse, unaccustomed to the unusual position of the man standing on the saddle, moved. She would not have had to move far for him to have lost his footing. When he slipped from the saddle his efforts to regain his footing would probably have disturbed her even more and once she moved away he was left swinging helplessly from the elbow.

One can imagine his feelings as he realised his awful predicament. No doubt he would have been in a state of mortal terror and a great deal of pain. It would have been impossible for him to get any sort of a foothold on the smooth bark of the gum tree and there was not a single branch or any kind of irregularity in the tree. Before long the pain must have been excruciating, the arm supporting, as it was, the entire weight of his body. He was about ten miles from his camp and there was no possibility of anyone being able to hear his cries for help. Of course, he would be well aware of this.

It would have been some time in mid-morning when he became trapped and minutes would have seemed like hours as time dragged by. He probably got to the stage when his reason was going and he imagined his dead body swinging from the elbow and being picked clean by voracious crows.

One can only guess how long he was helplessly hanging there. No doubt it was several hours. One can guess a little more accurately the state of his mind, semi-delirious with a desperation that knew no bounds. One can imagine him looking at the ground only a few feet away as he reached his absolute limit. He decided to sever his arm.

Like all bushmen he carried on his belt pouches containing a watch, matches for lighting a fire or his pipe and a knife, which all bushmen regard as indispensable.

He took his knife from the pouch on his belt and

started to cut his arm off at the shoulder making several deep cuts, but finding that too difficult, he then started to sever it at the elbow.

It is impossible to imagine what the poor fellow was going through as he continued his gruesome task and it is difficult to say how long it would have taken him to cut through with an ordinary pocket knife. It is reasonable to assume that the arm had lost all feeling. He would certainly have been hacking away at it for some time. Eventually he cut it through, fell to the ground, picked himself up, walked a few yards to the shade of a brigalow tree where he would have died in a few minutes from shock and loss of blood.

In the meantime, Tom Walsh, for whom Devaney was carting firewood and water, became increasingly worried at the continued absence of his team driver. The first thing a bushman would think of would be some kind of accident, perhaps due to his horse falling which was a fairly common occurrence. Perhaps he was lying out there incapacitated with a broken leg, or worse. On the other hand, there was a fencers' camp about eight miles away and, although he thought it was unlikely Devaney could have called there for a change of company and a yarn and having left it a bit late, decided to stay the night.

At about eleven o'clock he was so concerned that he woke his assistant and the two of them walked the eight miles, arriving there at one o'clock in the morning. To Walsh's consternation Alf Williams, the fencing contractor, told him that Devaney had certainly not been at his camp, so Walsh and Williams, together with Williams' men, a party of seven, set off in the direction they thought Devaney may have taken.

After travelling for a few miles cooee-ing loudly as they went, they heard barking and a few minutes later a small black and white dog ran to them. They immediately recognised Devaney's dog and followed it until they came to his body lying in the sandy bed of Wooroolah Creek.

At first glance Devaney appeared to be sleeping peacefully but on getting closer they saw, to their horror, that he was dead and had one arm missing. A trail of blood led them to the foot of a gum tree where his boots, hat, spurs and pocket knife were scattered around. Daylight was just beginning to break and they could see massive bloodstains standing out starkly on the white bark of the gum starting at a hole about ten feet up at a fork in the tree. It looked as though the tree had been discharging blood. One man stood on another's shoulders and put his arm into the hollow. One can imagine his horror on encountering three small parrots and part of a man's arm.

They then walked to a boundary rider's hut where there was a telephone and telephoned the grim news to the Manager, Mr O'Donahue, who in turn called the Blackall police constable, Thomas Chiconi. It was shortly after nine o'clock on the morning of October 22nd and as the policeman's only form of travel was by horse, it was late in the afternoon when the constable arrived at the station. He would have had to push his horse to have reached there in that time.

It is now appropriate for the Manager of Terrick Terrick to take up the story in a letter he wrote to Alf Devaney's brother in Sydney. In this letter he describes with great clarity the sequence of events from the discovery of the body up to the approaching magisterial enquiry. Here again my thanks are due to Mrs Cathy Beatty for obtaining a copy of the Manager's letter from the archives.

"TERRICK TERRICK"
BLACKALL. 24th Oct. 1912
Queensland.

Mr J. Devaney,
No. 2 Fitzroy Street,
Marrickville, Sydney.

Dear Sir,

On the 22nd inst. I sent a telegram to a Miss Devaney — presumably your own and the late Alf Devaney's sister — reading 'Deeply regret inform you that Alf Devaney met with fatal accident here yesterday. Writing' and I duly received your telegram in reply as follows 'Send corpse Sydney. All expenses paid here' to which I replied as follows: 'Absolutely impossible comply with your request body not found till at least sixteen hours after death 70 miles from nearest town. Heat intense must be buried immediately, could possibly exhume later on. Death caused by fall from tree whilst trying to get young birds.'

It appears that the unfortunate fellow took the saddle horse from the camp and rode it out about 8 miles to where he knew there was a galah's nest with young birds in it, and as he did not return, the Wellborer and his assistant went out about 11 pm to look for him. They first went to a fencing camp about 10 miles distant, thinking your brother may have gone there, but found that such was not the case. The fencing contractor and his men then joined in the search, making a party of seven. They had not gone more than a mile and a half, when the dog which your brother had with him came to them, as they were cooeeing, and they then went in the direction from which the dog came and found the deceased, lying on his back quite dead and cold, with one arm (the right one) missing. Searching around they found a quantity of blood round a tree twenty yards distant from the body, and on one of them

Court House
Blackall
29th October. 1912

Before A. B. Gibson Esq
Police Magistrate

Magisterial Inquiry held at
Blackall on Tuesday the
29th day of October 1912
touching the cause of death
of Alfred Devaney who met
his death by accident
at Terrick Terrick Station
near Blackall on Monday
the 21st day of October 1912

A B Gibson PM

Magistrate's report, 1912.

getting on the other's shoulders they found that the missing arm was in a hollow in the tree about 10ft from the ground. They then came in to a boundary rider's hut where we have a telephone, and telephoned the news to us at the head station. It was 4 am when the body was found and it was after 8 am when they got to the telephone a distance of about 10 miles, and we immediately telephoned to the Police at Blackall 42 miles distant.

A mounted constable came out but it was 6 p.m. by the time he got here, and I had a buggy and horses ready, and took him out to the place arriving there about 10 pm. We then got the arm out of the tree and from its appearance we concluded that it had been cut off with a knife and not torn off by the fall. We then carefully examined the body which was very much bruised and the examination confirmed the opinion that the arm had been cut off. The tree was a straight blue gum about 18 inches in diameter at the butt, and branched out into two at about 10 feet from the ground both limbs going nearly straight up and no other branches for some feet higher up. The hole in which the arm was found is right in the fork of the two limbs and is only about 3 inches by 5 inches being of an oval shape and the deceased having once got his arm into the hole and lost his footing had no possible chance of raising himself sufficiently to enable him to withdraw his arm. As far as we can judge, deceased must have stood up on the saddle and put his hand into the hollow to take the young birds out, and the mare — a very quiet old one must have moved or he slipped off the saddle and was thus left hanging by the arm, which must have been in the hole as far as the elbow. It is impossible to say how long the unfortunate fellow hung there, but there is no doubt he realised that his only hope was for some one to find him soon, or the only other alternative to cut his arm off and let himself down. There was a very remote chance of anyone finding him before the next day (Tuesday) even if then and he appears to have decided on the latter chance. He evidently tried at first to cut the arm off at the shoulder, as there was several long cuts on that joint, one of them being about an inch deep. Then he appears to have thought the elbow, which must have been just at the top of the hole — would be better and he managed to cut it clean through at that joint and let himself free. He then appears to have walked about 20 yards to the shade of some thick briglow trees and lied down, where, no doubt he must soon have died from loss of blood and shock.

The poor fellow does not seem to have suffered much after reaching the shade of the briglows, as there were not any signs of struggling, and he was lying on his back with his legs quite straight. But no doubt he must have suffered terrible agony up to the time he effected his release from the tree.

We buried him at midnight and the police took charge of his effects. I might mention that he was employed by me, carting wood and water for the engine used by the boring contractor to do the well boring with.

I have given you as much detail as I can thinking you and his other relatives would like to know as much about the poor fellow's end as possible and if there is anything in which I can be of service please do not hesitate to let me know. A magisterial enquiry is to be held on Tuesday next in Blackall and if you wish I will send you the newspaper report on it.

Yours faithfully,
H.M. O'Donahue

It is always interesting to speculate on the 'ifs' and 'buts', the 'what might have beens', of any situation. Alf

Devaney died and many people may think needlessly.

Had he not carried a knife he would have been unable to sever his arm. But when he did so, unquestionably he would have been in a state where his reason was gone. Had he been able to think straight he would have known that without any doubt, his mates would have started looking for him after some time had elapsed.

When he took that awful step it would be impossible for anyone to remotely imagine his suffering. At the inquest it was stated that his weight was twelve stone and it was that weight that his elbow joint was supporting. One can, however, imagine the feelings of his mates, their unstinting efforts in the middle of the night and their devastation when they found his body with the severed arm.

SPEARS AND
SMOKE SIGNALS

DARWIN HAS LONG ceased to be a far-flung outpost of
the British Empire, but for many years it was another
world where the flotsam and jetsam of humanity
drifted up, eddied around, got caught up or drifted off
again — a kaleidoscope of every creed and colour,
where East met West and only mediocrity stood out.
Pearlers rubbed shoulders with buffalo hunters, gold
miners swapped yarns with cattle men. The Chinese
smoked their opium, played mah-jong and minded
their own business.

The Darwin population stayed at around one thousand, including the Japanese indentured pearlers and
their Malay crewmen; Chinese storekeepers left over
from the railway line construction and their increasingly large families.

In 1928 two men arrived in Darwin — who became
friends. Jim Nichols, an itinerant station worker and
Jack Renault, an Australian of French extraction.
Renault, the younger man, confided to Nichols that he

intended to buy a boat, sail around the coast and hopefully, write a book. Renault's enthusiasm was infectious. He asked Nichols to join him and he readily agreed — no persuasion was needed. He would go with him perhaps as far as Broome, but first a boat had to be found. A week later Renault had found what he wanted, a trim little twenty-five foot sailing boat. The two men put her up on the beach, cleaned her down and painted her. When the boat was ready they floated her off on a high tide, loaded up with provisions and left, beating into the south-east trades, idling along and putting into various inlets as fancy took them.

Daly River Aborigines.

They passed the mouth of the Finniss River, rounded Point Blaze and anchored. A minor caulking job had to be done. It was only a simple job, a couple of planks needed attention, and it was a matter of waiting for the right tide so that the little craft could be beached and safely floated off again. In those latitudes at the time of the spring tides the rise and fall was sometimes in excess of twenty-five feet. If beached at the wrong time a boat could lie there for months.

The next day, Renault casually announced that he was going ashore to shoot a few ducks or geese. From their anchorage, he could see a lagoon of some sort, from which birds could be seen rising. Renault cleaned the protective coating from the gun as they rusted quickly in that climate if not cared for. Nichols rowed him ashore in their little dinghy and returned to the boat where he busied himself with odd jobs as there was always something to do. Some time later, he heard a shot — they would have a good meal that night he thought — shortly afterwards, another shot reverberated across the water.

Nichols watched the shore for his mate's return, but two hours later there was still no sign of Renault and he began to feel uneasy. After a while he rowed ashore, beached the dinghy and walked in the direction from where he heard the shots. It wasn't far to the lagoon. Circling kite hawks led him to the water.

Renault was dead. A shovel spear had pierced his chest — two dead geese lay beside him — there was no sign of the gun. He had been speared at the water's edge. It appeared as though he had gone into the water to retrieve the birds leaving his gun on the bank and a native had crept up and, hidden by tall rushes that skirted the lagoon, killed him and taken the gun.

Nichols was stunned by what had happened. It was two days sail back to Darwin under favourable conditions, but he had to leave his friend's body there as it would have been illegal to have buried him. All kinds of formalities had to be completed, the police would have to be informed and a coronial enquiry would have to take place.

He went back to the boat and returned with an axe, cutting a quantity of bushes, doing his best to cover the body completely although he knew that dingoes would be tearing at it as soon as decomposition set in, if not before. He sailed back to Darwin with the tragic news and the wheels of officialdom ground into gear. A boat left Darwin with police and a coroner who found that Jack Renault had died from spear wounds inflicted by persons unknown. At the same time Mounted Constable Tom Hemmings set out with horses, trackers and enough rations to last a month. Three weeks later he returned, one of his trackers had two spear wounds, he had no prisoners and the wet season had set in. The smoke signals had spoken their message.

Bullita Station, a two thousand square mile cattle property on the East Baines River, always had its problems. Beyond the blood-red escarpments where the river headed was the home of a tribe of nomad Aboriginals who made regular forays into the Bullita herds grazing on the river flats.

In 1929 I was the manager with ten stock boys, a jackeroo of limited ability and a cook. My problem at this particular time was not so much the spearing of my cattle as the loss of my cook who suddenly made a lightning decision to depart for greener fields. Men were few and far between in that very isolated neck of the woods and I dreaded the thought of transferring the jackeroo to the post. As durable as my constitution was I doubted its ability to cope with such a drastic change.

Miracles do happen and a few days later a man rode up to the homestead looking for work. It was Jim Nichols. I knew of him of course, and his involvement with Renault. He didn't want the cooking job, he wanted yard building or fencing. I had some of that too, but I talked him into the cooking job until I got someone.

Some time later I got a cook and the next day Nichols and I rode out to his first job, repairing a stock yard on Fig Tree Creek. It was known as Crisp's Yard, named after a previous manager, Jim Crisp, who had been speared some years earlier. I showed Nichols what I wanted done, a few rails replaced and a gate renewed. After looking at the job we walked over to where Jim Crisp was buried. It was almost trampled out of sight by cattle and as an afterthought I told him to tidy up the grave and put a few rails round to keep the cattle off.

Nichols never alluded to the Renault killing until one night, over a bottle of rum, he opened up somewhat. It had affected him very deeply as he had clearly developed a sincere liking for the younger man. Some weeks later he finished the last job. I would have liked to have kept him on, he was a useful man to have around, but my finances were restricted and I just didn't have any funds to spare — so he left.

It was nearly twelve months before I heard of him again — the bush telegraph drummed its message — Jim Nichols had been speared on Mainoru Station, an isolated property on the edge of Arnhem Land where he had been building a stockyard.

Superintendent Alf Stretton was the Chief of the Northern Territory Mounted Police and was admirably suited to the post. He was born at Borooloola where his father was a sergeant of police. His knowledge of the Northern Territory and its problems was unparalleled and his bailiwick, by any standards, was of considerable proportions. From its southern border to the outlying islands in the Arafura Sea was about twelve hundred miles, from east to west was more than five hundred and, within those boundaries, there were swamps, jungles, mountains, unmapped rivers and waterless deserts, a lot of it difficult access. The few roads, such as they were meandering across the country, were impassable in the wet season, even for horses.

Stretton's force numbered thirty-two men with whom he administered law and order over five hundred and twenty-three thousand square miles. Excluding Darwin he had eighteen police posts, most of which were manned by one mounted constable and a couple of black trackers. Their only means of transport was by horse and sometimes they would be on patrol for weeks on end. In the wet season they were paralysed by flooded rivers and bog to the eyebrows. Apart from the few stations on the Overland Telegraph Line none of them had any form of communication, ignorance was most certainly bliss.

The early thirties were vintage years for the spearmen of the north. Herb Watts was speared at Hermit Hill close to the Daly River and Bill Telow was killed not far away. Then the lugger *Pat* was attacked. Mounted Constable Jack Kennett was aboard on his way to Timber Creek Police Station, to where he had been transferred when he was badly cut by a tomahawk. He was the only casualty.

A pearling lugger, the *Ouida*, sailed into the aptly named Treachery Bay on August 1931. The captain, a Japanese named Nagata, was killed with his own gun and the other Japanese, Yoshia and Owashi, were tomahawked to death. It was months before the news filtered through to Darwin and by then the wet had set in. But one thing seemed certain — the culprits were Nemarluk and some fellow tribesmen.

As soon as the wet took up, two of Stretton's most experienced men set out from the Daly River Police

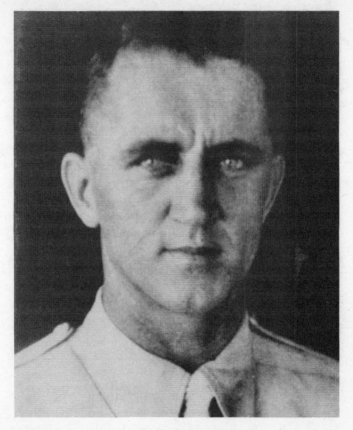

Jack Mahoney.

Post. Fred Don and Bill McCann were well-equipped with sixteen saddle horses and six others to carry the packs, two months rations, two black trackers and two horse boys. Their orders were to bring Nemarluk back. They never got anywhere near him but they did catch Widjulli, the man who speared Herb Watts, some sort of consolation prize. Worst of all, they lost one of their best saddle horses which was taken by a crocodile while crossing the Fitzmaurice River.

In May of the same year, 1932, Constable Ted Morey and Jack Mahoney were stationed at Timber Creek and they too joined the hunt for Nemarluk. Then more bad news came in. Two prospectors, Stephens and Cook, left the coastal vessel *Maroubra* at the mouth of the Fitzmaurice River. They had a big canoe which they had made themselves and ample supplies. Their intentions were to go up the Fitzmaurice as far as possible and prospect for gold in the Mt Barwolla area. They didn't get very far. Two days later Nemarluk and his merry men speared them, chopped them up and threw the bodies to the crocodiles — there were plenty of them.

Morey and Mahoney left their Timber Creek Station with three trackers, eighteen horses and eight pack mules. They splashed across the Victoria River and crossed the Ikymbon River the next day. Smoke signals rose into the cloudless sky. Six weeks later they had caught Marragin, one of Nemarluk's tribesmen, but by then they had run out of rations and so made their way back to Brocks Creek and took the weekly train to Darwin.

Constable Tas Fitzer took up the hunt with Bul-Bul, the best black tracker in the north, and this time Nemarluk felt the cold grip of handcuffs. Fitzer brought him to Darwin together with an assortment of his countrymen who had no hesitation testifying against him. He was duly convicted and, at the conclusion of the trial, several of the witnesses requested to go to jail also. Through an interpreter they explained that they would not expect any pay. This however was refused. Three months later Nemarluk escaped. It seemed that it was a lot easier to get out than it was to get in.

Pearling was very much in the doldrums in the early thirties and many of the luggers of Darwin fleets were turning to trepang, a Malay word for beche-de-mer, the slug of the sea, a delicacy highly prized by the gourmets of the East. It is plentiful on the shallow reefs of our northern coastline and is gathered by diving, then it is boiled and smoked.

In September 1932, two luggers, the *Raf* and the *Myrtle Olga* manned by Japanese and Melville Island natives, left Darwin, sailed along the Arnhem Land coast and turned into Caledon Bay. They anchored close ashore, set up boilers and smokehouses and started to dive for trepang.

Melville Island, Northern Territory

The Balamumu tribe of that area were probably the most primitive in Australia, very few could even speak pidgin English. They lived by hunting and fishing, made fire by rubbing two sticks together and their weapons were spears which they would fit into a woomera and drive with tremendous force and accuracy. The Japanese were not entirely new to them as luggers would frequently put in for fresh water. The tribe cautiously approached them. Tukiar, a warrior of

Constable McColl, starting his last camel patrol in May 1932.

some standing, sent one of his wives with barramundi he had speared in exchange for tobacco and matches. Smoke signals curled upwards and gleaming black warriors arrived and peered at the industrious Japanese from the adjacent jungle.

The Japanese were creatures of habit and worked methodically — at certain times they would all be ashore at once. Tukiar and his warriors sharpened their spears and one morning swept into the camp and speared them all. It was quite simple. They then looted the luggers which was even simpler. The Melville Islanders escaped, they may even have been forewarned.

Traynor and Fagan were two young men who had drifted into Darwin. Both being of an adventurous nature they had built themselves a boat — not A1 at Lloyds but it did float. They sailed north-east, rounded the Coburg Peninsula, passed through the Wessel Island group and, about a month after the Japanese were murdered, turned into Blue Mud Bay. They were in Tukiar's country. Again the smoke signals spoke their language and again, fortified by his last success, Tukiar gathered his warriors together and fitted their spears into their woomeras. Traynor and Fagan were killed at sunrise and their bodies thrown into the sea.

The news worked its way through the bush tele-graph system slowly. The Roper River Police Post was the first to hear of it and, although very garbled, it was clear that there had been some multiple murders. Superintendent Stretton had plenty on his plate. There were murderers footloose in the swamps of the lower Daly River, there were murderers roaming the lower reaches of the Victoria River and there were murder-ers enjoying life somewhere in Arnhem Land. The stories were building up too with the most pressing appearing to be the Arnhem Land killings. Nothing could be done for a week or so, the rivers were still raging torrents pouring out of the sandstone escarp-ments and the country was impassable. But the patrol could be got ready.

Stretton had no hesitation earmarking the men for

Patrol patrol. (Photo courtesy of Mrs K. Morey)

the job. Ted Morey was undoubtedly the best man he had and he would be the leader. He was an outstanding horseman, a more than competent bushman and a natural leader. Vic Hall, another good man, would go and Jack Mahoney and Bert McColl would complete the team.

They left the small township of Katherine with twenty-five good saddle horses and eight pack mules loaded with stores and supplies. There were four trackers, two more were to be picked up at the Roper River Police Post which would be their last contact before they set off into the trackless wilds. With additional horses from Roper they had 56 and 15 packs.

From there they arranged for a Mission launch, the *Holly*, to take Vic Hall and Bert McColl round by sea. They were to rendezvous in the vicinity of Caledon Bay. Morey and Mahoney had a hard trek by land and left first taking two weeks to get to the coast. They met as arranged and they all knew that there was no chance of surprising Tukiar and his fellow tribesmen. As they were approaching the coast they had seen smoke signals rising every day.

Some preliminary scouting around soon disclosed that there were no Aboriginals obligingly waiting to be arrested or even interviewed and what tracks were there were at least a week old. There were signs of canoes on the beach, but only signs. They moved to Blue Mud Bay and made their first contact with two old men who, on questioning, vaguely pointed seaward.

Leaving the horses in charge of trackers they embarked on the *Holly* and went to Round Hill Island. Here there were plenty of tracks, canoes had been beached recently, but they had left within the last day or so. From there they went to Woodah Island which was densely timbered, about forty miles long and per-

haps ten miles wide at its widest. There were fresh
tracks in abundance and later on they found some
canoes drawn up in a creek. Not far away they surprised four lubras but were unable to get much information from them. They couldn't or wouldn't speak
pidgin or English but they understood the name of
Tukiar, that much was clear. By impounding the
canoes Morey decided that at least he would have
them bottled up on the island, but it was a big island
and their difficulties were compounded by the dense
scrub.

Morey left McColl to watch the canoes and also the
women who were handcuffed. Two trackers stayed
with him while Morey, Hall and Mahoney took one
tracker each and set out in an endeavour to locate
Tukiar and his followers. The three policemen met up
at sundown and as they were too far away to get back
to where they left McColl they camped in the bush.
What little food they had taken with them had been
eaten and they had no camping equipment so they
were very hungry and uncomfortable that night.

When daylight broke they made back to where

A group of Aborigines. (Photo courtesy of Mrs K. Morey)

JULY 1935

19 FRIDAY 200-165

Returned to camp with
one pack load of oats &
one pack load of fodder
Boys returned to camp
with dray load of salt
& rations

20 SATURDAY 201-164

Put eight horses down the ylown
for a spell. & shot. six buffalo

21 SUNDAY 202-163
5th Sunday after Trinity

Shot up the Wildman & got eleven
hides. Saw a lot of smoke signals
of blacks going across from
Wildman to Flying Fox & sent Jack
up to try & intercept then but he
failed to do so

Entries from Tom Cole's diaries.

they had left McColl, the two trackers and prisoners. Shortly after sunrise they heard two shots and they pressed on as fast as they could. They arrived at where they had left McColl and the others, but there was no one there — no sign of the policeman, the trackers or the lubras. Morey and his party immediately set out in search. Calling loudly they split up and circled around — it was one of the trackers who found Bert McColl. He was dead. A shovel spear had gone through his chest and he would have died instantly. Two cartridges in his revolver had been discharged.

It took some time for the shock of the tragedy to sink in. They buried McColl. Morey decided that they would have to return to Darwin and report the murder of their fellow officer. It was a sorry party that made their way back. When Morey, Mahoney and Hall got to Darwin all hell broke loose. There was immediate talk of a punitive expedition, but that was quickly knocked on the head. The missionaries, fearing with some justification a wholesale massacre, stepped in and offered to bring the murderers in. Superintendent Stretton, with no doubt some pressure from the South, agreed, thinking privately that they would be unsuccessful. However, to everyone's astonishment, missionaries from Millingimbi Island brought in Tukiar and some of his countrymen.

The ensuing court case was something of a shambles. Most of the witnesses seemed to have no idea what it was all about, very few could even speak pidgin, and the interpreters weren't much better. Tukiar was found not guilty and discharged but he never reached his country. What happened to him was a matter of speculation.

Nemarluk was more fortunate. He was re-arrested and brought back to Fanny Bay jail where, one assumes, he lived happily ever after as he died in jail. A

Darwin street is named after him which must surely be unique.

Ted Morey was invalided out of the police in 1947 due to a heart condition and for the next few years he engaged in crocodile hunting. Some years later he retired to Adelaide and during his declining years he was horse breaking for the well-known trainer Bart Cummings.

FLYING

FENTON, M.D.

THE FIRST DOCTOR to practise in the Northern Territory was Surgeon Woods. He was assigned to a detachment of King George IV's Third Regiment of Foot, the famous *Buffs* commanded by Major Campbell, which was stationed in 1824 on Melville Island.

It is extremely doubtful if the good doctor would have chosen to practise in such a far-flung outpost of the Empire but, having taken the king's shilling, it was not his to reason why. His surgery was a thatched hut, his tools of trade were saws, searing irons, knives and pincers. His medicines were cinchona bark, vinegar, castor oil and mysterious physics and potions not far removed from those used by the witch doctors peering from the surrounding jungle.

Surgeon Woods' tour of duty was a brief and unhappy one, voluntarily terminated while he was stricken with malaria. In the black depression which overtakes sufferers of this tropical curse he cut his own throat.

He was succeeded by Surgeon Gold, described by contemporaries as a 'foppish man, all ringlets and ruffles, given to quoting French and Latin.' Gold's duration was even shorter than that of his predecessor. Walking in the forest one evening he and John Green, the storekeeper, died in a hail of spears unleashed with horrifying savagery. The surgeon's body was pierced with thirty-one of the most lethal shafts ever devised by primitive man. The storekeeper took nearly twenty and had his skull crushed by a nulla-nulla to make up for the deficiency of missiles.

Disregarding the indigenous practitioners, who are just as active today, there have been none since who have had their names inscribed in the history books — with one notable exception. That exception was Australia's first Flying Doctor. In fact, he was probably Australia's only Flying Doctor, by which I mean that he bought his own aeroplanes, he flew his own aeroplanes and he wrecked his own aeroplanes — without any help from anyone else.

In the Northern Territory he was revered from Darwin to Alice Springs, from Wyndham to Camooweal. He was idolised by men who knew all about overwhelming odds. He was not the original nonconformist, but he certainly improved on their lifestyle. He broke just about every flying regulation known, and a few that weren't. The Department of Civil Aviation regarded him as a thorn in their collective sides though he wasn't really — he was a bloody great spike. And all because he never flew by the book nor followed the rules. In spite of all this he relieved more suffering and saved more lives than the rest of the Health Department combined.

He was an extraordinary man in so many respects and one of the few people to whom that overworked term, 'nature's gentleman', could be truly applied. He was kind, gentle, and compassionate, with an irrepressible sense of humour, and he smoked the most powerful cigars I've ever nearly choked on. His name was Clyde Cornwall Fenton.

A mail boat nosed its way alongside the Darwin wharf, its engines reversing as the mooring lines were picked up and the looped ends dropped over bollards. It was low tide and the scene was far from salubrious. Across the mud flats on the distant beach several luggers were standing in temporary cradles undergoing careening, while half a dozen others swung at anchor where the flats shelved down into deeper water. Darwin was an active pearling port.

On the upper deck passengers peered across the dank stretch of mud to an eminence almost a mile away where a few buildings could be seen peeping through a fringe of poinsettia trees blazing with crimson. The tides went out a long way in those latitudes, the rise and fall being something in the vicinity of twenty-five feet.

Among the passengers lining the rail was a tousle-haired, bespectacled young man. He was Clyde Fenton, until recently the Government Medical Officer at the port of Wyndham in Western Australia, on his way to Melbourne and looking forward to a well-earned holiday. He waved enthusiastically to one of the group gathered on the wharf, a figure of somewhat striking appearance, standing over six feet in height and, although barely forty, displaying a shock of snow-white hair above eyes of an almost startling blueness. At first glance he almost appeared to have a squint. Certainly there was something that could cause the recipient of a fixed stare some uneasiness. There was, of course, a simple explanation for this. Cecil Evelyn Cook, known to friends as 'Mick' the Northern Territory's Chief Medical Officer, had a glass eye.

When the gangway was secured Fenton was one of the first ashore and the two men drove off together. At this point, events became somewhat obscure and for a very good reason. There was a Northern Territory reunion of massive proportions which, gentle readers and others, you can rightly assume to have been of a couple of days duration at least. And although most certainly what followed was not intended with malice, there were undoubtedly overtones of aforethought because when Fenton came out of his alcoholic daze his luggage was neatly stacked beside him in Cook's spare bedroom and the ship had sailed.

The host was fairly frank about it. After all, he could afford to be, because there wasn't another ship for a month and it was going to Singapore anyway. He pleaded his case with eloquence fortified by the shipping situation and the approaching wet season. The one road out of Darwin was only traversable under very favourable conditions. True, there was a railway line with a train and all, but it only went as far as Birdum, a terrible place to be marooned where there wasn't even a pub.

The fact of the matter was that Dr Cook was just about at the end of his tether. He was Chief Medical Officer with four hospitals, two of which had to be staffed by nurses. His only doctor was nine hundred miles away at Alice Springs. In addition to the administrative side of his position and his personal attention at the hospital, he was a Justice of the Peace and also saddled with the dubious distinction of being Chief Protector of Aborigines. The arrival of another doctor was an answer to his prayers.

Fenton's grasp of the situation was immediate. Apart from the bonds of friendship he was one whose susceptibilities, particularly in that area, were very sensitive. Even if an escape route had been available, he would not have taken it. He stayed for five months, four of them during the wet season when everything was immobilised. Even horses were unable to plough through the black quagmire once the wet really set in. His feelings of helplessness were intensified when word came through the grapevine of women in childbirth difficulties, or a case of appendicitis. A broken leg or arm weren't too bad and a broken neck was usually final. When he was preparing to leave Katherine he told Cook that he would come back and bring an aeroplane.

His interest and fascination with aeroplanes had begun when he served in the Royal Air Force in England as a medical officer, and he had no difficulty talking his way into some *ex officio* flying lessons. From then on he was hooked. But an aeroplane in the Northern Territory in 1929!! That was beyond the realms of fantasy!

He boarded the *Marella* and at the top of the gangway he turned and called to the cluster of people who had come to farewell him, 'I'll see you at Fanny Bay.' That might have been misinterpreted by a stranger because Fanny Bay was the location of Darwin Jail. Only recently had the paddock between the corrective institution and the shoreline been adopted as a landing ground for the new breed of intrepid adventurers blazing fresh trails in the sky — Kingsford Smith, Amy Johnson, Bert Hinkler and others.

Clyde Fenton had planned to be back in six months but, as a well-known Scottish bard with a tendency to immortalise rodents, said, 'The best laid plans of mice and men...' (The remainder of the quotation is in a strange language with which I am not familiar.) The Great Depression swept remorselessly across the world engulfing Australia, and, although Fenton could have returned to the Territory and taken up where he left off, it would have been without an aeroplane. This had become almost an obsession.

It was not until 1933 that Fenton was able to make definite plans, and even then there were numerous obstacles and frustrations, not the least of which was money. A doctor's salary at that time was eight pounds a week. Although terrified at the thought of her son flying, his mother lent him some money and, when a mining company weighed in with another loan, his dream was realised. He bought a Gypsy Moth for five hundred pounds. Today that may seem an insignificant sum for an aeroplane but to get it into some sort of perspective it must be remembered that, during the Depression years, a good three-bedroom house could be bought for a few hundred pounds and a choice building block in a select area for twenty.

Fenton's appointment to the Northern Territory Medical Service was automatic but Dr Cook experienced some difficulty persuading the panjandrums of Canberra to grant allowance for the aeroplane. Determined to maintain their reputation for parsimony towards the Territory, they reluctantly agreed to an allowance of one hundred pounds a year for maintenance, plus one shilling for every mile he flew — exactly the same rate that was paid for motor car hire.

With a red cross emblazoned on each side of the plane beside the registration UNI, he took off from Essendon aerodrome in Victoria, full of the joy of living and reached Darwin four days later. A new era had begun.

The Northern Territory was in reality governed from Canberra and the Administrator, Colonel Weddell, was more or less a figurehead who was there to do as he was told. He was under The Department of Territories and the relationship had always been one of mutual distrust. However, Weddell was experienced and familiar enough with the ways of politicians to know that the best policy to adopt was to let lying dogs sleep. His career was drawing to a close anyway — all he wanted was a quiet life.

The Medical Service was in a much stronger position, having a fair amount of autonomy. This was largely due to Dr Cook's personality, but the protective mystique the medical profession has always found useful to maintain contributed to the service's independence. Nevertheless, lack of funds was always a heartbreaking problem. The Depression had by no means loosened its grip, although the Territory, because of the resourcefulness of those who lived there, was better off than other states.

When it came to such matters as money for a few aerodromes Canberra wasn't sure whether the Chief Medical Officer was out of his mind or just trying to be funny — funny ha-ha and funny peculiar too. What on earth was the matter with him? Wasn't the Northern Territory a land of wide open spaces?

Katherine, which took its name from the river on which the township had grown up, became the new Flying Doctor's base. It was reasonably central to the more settled part, by which I mean the population was about two to the thousand square miles as against .002 a couple of hundred miles to the south. Furthermore, the Overland Telegraph Line ran through the town and the hospital was hooked up to it — although it was sometimes a bit difficult breaking through the sound barrier of the party line. 'Like a tree full of bloody parrots,' Fenton told Cook. There was a train too, affectionately known as 'Leaping Lena', which left Darwin on Wednesday, stayed the first night at Pine Creek and made a midday stop at Katherine on Thursday. From there it went to Birdum where it had

Dr Fenton's plane when he landed near the Tennant Creek Post Office to take a sick man to Alice Springs.

another night's rest before starting the return journey on Friday — again staying overnight at Pine Creek and struggling into Darwin on Saturday afternoon. The six hundred miles there and back in four days was a real endurance test.

The new Flying Doctor was very quickly in business and the Government, as is the fashion of governments, intended to get their money's worth. He was frequently called upon to do charter work, which might be termed beyond the call of duty. However, Fenton had no objection whatever to doing this. After all, he was not only getting a shilling a mile but increasing his knowledge of the country.

And so it came about that he was required to fly one Dr Woolnough, an eminent geologist, round the country. Woolnough was fairly well known and could look after himself in the bush, but he was likely to turn up anywhere once he started following a likely looking reef. Fenton had dropped the geologist off and gone on to attend to a patient a couple of hundred miles away. When he returned a couple of days later, Woolnough had gone off in an entirely different direction to an entirely different place. Woolnough's attitude was, 'He'll find me.'

A drover with a thousand head of bullocks was more than a little surprised when an aeroplane landed beside his feeding cattle. Assuming that the pilot was in some kind of trouble, he cantered over to the aeroplane anxiously to ask if the pilot was all right. Climbing from the cockpit, Fenton explained that he was looking for Dr Woolnough. The drover scratched his head and said he'd never heard of any doctor round the country, although right then he could do with one because he had a raging toothache. Fenton explained that although Woolnough was a rock doctor, he himself was the other kind and could extract the offending molar. He had no dental equipment with him, however, and would fly the man to Wyndham, pull the tooth and fly him back next day.

No good, said the drover. He was too short-handed to leave the cattle. He rummaged around in a packbag and produced a pair of fencing pliers. 'What's wrong with these?' he asked 'Well,' Fenton said, 'If you're game I certainly am.' The bushman sat down on a log and with his back to a tree told him to go ahead. When the operation was finished the old cattleman wrapped the tooth in a filthy handkerchief, put it in his pocket and rode after his cattle.

Dr Fenton climbed into the cockpit of his aeroplane to continue his search for the elusive 'rock doctor', eventually running him to earth at Mistake Creek, an outstation of Ord River Station. It was the night of a full moon in a cloudless sky which was, as it turned out, unfortunate. They decided to fly to Wave Hill about two hundred miles away. There wasn't much in the way of landmarks in the daytime let alone at night, and when Wave Hill failed to materialise Fenton started to get worried. After all, flying an aeroplane around the Northern Territory in the middle of the night in 1934 with no navigational aids, no airstrips, no anything much, was not conducive to a peaceful frame of mind.

The fuel gauge was relentlessly working its way towards zero when Clyde Fenton decided he was lost. He was a very brave man, something he proved over and over again, but that night his nerves of chilled steel were tested. He knew he had to land very soon and, with one eye on the fuel gauge, he circled anxiously looking for a clearing where he could put the aeroplane down with a reasonable chance of surviving.

He selected an area which, as far as he could see and judge with the moon casting strange shadows, gave them that chance. He sat the aircraft down and, although there was an almighty crash, it came to rest a bit lopsided in a shallow hole. They scrambled out from their cockpits and an immediate examination disclosed no damage, or at any rate nothing that was obvious. A more detailed inspection at daybreak confirmed the aircraft was undamaged. The fuel gauge was registering sufficient fuel for fifteen or twenty minutes flying, which Fenton decided would be enough to get him either to Wave Hill or Victoria River Downs. He knew that once he sighted the Victoria River, which couldn't be far away, he could get his bearings. But he would have to leave Woolnough on the ground. The impromptu airstrip was not long enough for a safe take-off carrying a passenger. In any case, the 'rock doctor's' enthusiasm for flying with Fenton was somewhat diminished and it was probably with some relief that he found himself grounded.

Woolnough swung the propeller and the engine caught and fired. After a warming up period, Fenton taxied back as far as possible and gunned the motor. The plane rocked its way across the ground and, after about three hundred yards, rose effortlessly, clearing the trees comfortably with perhaps a hundred feet to spare. At an altitude of about five hundred feet, the Flying Doctor was astonished to see a group of buildings, the roofs reflecting the rays of the rising sun, no more than seven or eight miles away. It was Victoria River Downs. Overjoyed at the sight, Fenton decided to scribble a note to Woolnough. He swooped low, threw the piece of paper over the side and made another turn to make sure his companion on the ground had seen it. A wing clipped a tree and the whole world exploded.

Woolnough was horrified. The aeroplane was upside down, the wheels sticking up in the air, one wing missing and the remaining one waving in the wind. There was no sign of the pilot. With an overbearing sense of tragedy he ran across to the wreckage, and was astonished and overjoyed to see Fenton emerging from the pile of crumpled metal — as he expressed it, 'Like toothpaste coming out of a tube that had been trodden on.'

Fenton wrote later, 'Everything that I had hoped and dreamed, planned and schemed, for seven long years to achieve, and now after a brief two months the fruits of all my labours, all my hopes, lay in a shattered, twisted wreck. All I had was a crippling debt.' It is easy to appreciate his sense of tragedy. Some years later he quoted Rudyard Kipling's lines:

> If you can meet with triumph and disaster and treat these two impostors just the same.

The only part of that with which I don't agree is that disaster was never an impostor — ever.

At any rate, the two warriors now knew where they were. They walked to Victoria River Downs Station, where they were given a somewhat stunned and sorrowful welcome. The manager, Alf Martin, drove them to Katherine, from where they made their way to Darwin by train.

Fenton's immediate concern was another aeroplane. Since he had by this time demonstrated its value, Dr Cook backed him all the way. The Queensland and Northern Territory Aerial Services, having expanded considerably and acquired the acronym of 'Qantas', were running a service as far as Camooweal on the Northern Territory border. Fenton's SOS reached their ears and they let him know they had a Gypsy Moth for sale at six hundred pounds. All very well, but the last one wasn't paid for.

Then Fenton tried the Federal Government who, after they got over the initial shock of such unparalleled impertinence, asked how they would recover their money in the rather likely event of the eminent doctor getting killed. He jumped that hurdle by offering to assign his life insurance policy. The most remarkable feature of this was that actually he had one. He must have sneaked up on some unsuspecting insurance company when they weren't looking.

But the next high jump wasn't so easy. The Department of Civil Aviation, as any one of its numerous personnel would tell you, was about three jumps ahead of Jesus Christ — and don't you forget it either. Fenton was asked to show cause why his flying licence shouldn't be cancelled, given that he'd been landing aeroplanes all over the place where there were no aerodromes, crashing in the middle of the night without permission, and coming out alive without permission too! For a while it looked serious — an aeroplane and no licence to fly, because the powers that be in Canberra were still chewing the cud over the six hundred quid.

It took some time, and the combined efforts of Dr Cook and Dr Woolnough to get him off the hook. A part-Aboriginal woman helped. She was trying to have a baby but it got stuck halfway. Fenton flew off to get the maternity case fixed up. By the time he got back he had another aeroplane and owed for nearly two. The registration letters of the new plane was VH-UOI, which forever after he referred to as IOU.

His record of flying hours from then on was nothing short of dizzy. There was a flight to Alice Springs, 900 miles mostly at night, to treat a man with tetanus, then to Victoria River Downs to repair someone who had had an unsuccessful encounter with a mad bull. Then he was off to Ord River where a commercial plane had crash-landed and had a dead passenger and a badly mangled pilot and to Millingimbi Island to pick up an epileptic — an epileptic in a Gypsy Moth!!

Then came more trouble with his enemy which he had christened The Department of Uncivil Aviation. Arriving in Darwin one Saturday night after sundown while circling to land, he happened to spy the silver screen of the open air theatre rising above the surrounding roofs, depicting a torrid love scene which was far too good to miss. The next half hour was spent endeavouring, as he put it, 'to improve my technique.'

It didn't take long for the Wrath of God to descend in the shape of a telegram:

> Your pilot's Licence No 1221 is suspended until further notice Stop Certificate of airworthiness of your aircraft VH-UOI is suspended until such time as navigation lights are fitted.

Well that wasn't as bad as it seemed. A good hard look at the various licences revealed that Licence No 1221 was a private licence that had expired and had not been renewed because he had taken out a commercial licence. However, if DCA couldn't have a pound of flesh they would settle for half a pound. He was fined twenty pounds for low flying and another twenty when his appeal failed.

His aeroplane was now showing signs of strain and needed some attention. Qantas, now Qantas Empire Airways, had a base in Darwin and arrangements were made for an essential overhaul. It would take forty-eight hours. But Fenton not having an aeroplane in working order didn't stop people getting sick and having accidents. An urgent telegram from the Roper River Mission was the first bad news. A young Aboriginal boy had been so badly burned, the artery walls in his legs were in danger of bursting. Their telegram to the Australian Inland Mission aerial ambulance stationed at Cloncurry was no help. A very prompt reply regretfully refused because the Roper River Mission aerodrome was unlicensed! So much for that lot who were the recipients of substantial public donations.

Fenton was shocked and outraged. It was a measure of his dedication that he approached the representatives of a failed mining company which had a Gypsy Moth for sale at four hundred and fifty pounds, but they wanted cash, or perhaps a substantial guarantee. The Administrator, Colonel Weddell, was dragged out of bed. Would he as representative of the Commonwealth Government guarantee the amount? Well, he'd have to see what his masters in Canberra had to say about the matter. It was pointed out that the boy would most likely be dead before they got a reply — how would he feel about that? He signed and went back to bed. The aeroplane, VH-UJN, which had previously been christened, perhaps with a certain amount of unwarranted optimism, 'The Magic Carpet', was wheeled out of the hanger. The doctor climbed into the cockpit, warmed the engine while waiting for daylight, then headed for the Roper River Mission. There was no question about the seriousness of the case. Some arteries had to be tied before the boy could be lifted into the aeroplane and, although he recovered, he was two years in hospital.

Then came the bombshell from Canberra. The Government repudiated the Administrator's guarantee with some sharp knuckle-rapping thrown in. This was indeed an indescribable tangle. Fenton's first aeroplane, UNI, still wasn't paid for, nor was IOU, scattered over Qantas workshop floor, and 'The Magic Carpet' was now unguaranteed. All the people down the line who were hoping to get their money some day were down on their hands and knees busy praying to various deities to keep him alive. He certainly needed a powerful guardian angel.

He kept flying. An Aboriginal stockman with a spear through his chest and a miner badly buckled after getting in the way of some falling rock were additional emergencies. A shooting at a Tennant Creek gold field over a simple matter of claim jumping provided a diversion too. One of the participants, Snowy Renfrey, I knew quite well. He was quite a tough character and had had his face carved up some time previously in a difference of opinion over a card game. His assailant had meant to cut Snowy's throat but his aim wasn't too good and anyway Snowy did his best to avoid it. The scars that resulted from that encounter were quite spectacular. The gold miner who wanted to shoot Snowy was called O'Brien. The dispute about the claim must have been common knowledge because Snowy was in the bar when someone told him that O'Brien was coming and had a rifle. Snowy walked out on to the verandah of the hotel with his rifle, a Winchester 32.40, and called to O'Brien who was still some distance away. 'Here I am. Have a bloody shot!'

The two men took aim at the same time, Snowy saying, 'A long shot for a good man.' O'Brien, struck by two bullets, fell badly wounded.

The two trained nurses at the Australian Inland Mission immediately sent for Fenton, but O'Brien died before the doctor arrived. Snowy Renfrey was fined for carrying a firearm in a public place. Law and order had arrived at Tennant Creek.

As a postscript to the above story, many years later I was in Madang in New Guinea when, to my astonishment, Snowy Renfrey walked into the hotel where I was staying. He hadn't changed much in the thirty years since I'd seen him last and the scar on his cheek was a predominant feature of his landscape. I suppose I hadn't changed that much either. We went to the bar, of course, and went over old tracks and blazed a few new trails, too. Although I would have liked to at least touch on the shooting of O'Brien it would have been bad manners to have done so. Towards evening though one of those lulls occurred, as happens in all conversations, and suddenly Snowy looked up from the glass he had been contemplating. 'You know Tom,' he said, 'I had to shoot that bastard.' Nothing more. I just nodded and called for another drink.

Snowy left the next morning, and I never saw or heard of him again. I thought he was quite a good bloke.

At Katherine one evening a call came from Manbulloo Station which was purely social. Johnny Newmarch, the manager, suggested the doctor come over for a game of bridge — 'Bring Sister Lord too.' It was nearly dark when they left for Katherine. Fenton had been assured that the aerodrome would be illuminated with Newman's car headlights, but the station manager got tangled up with some logs and when Fenton made his approach the car headlights were pointing the wrong way. There was nothing magic about 'Magic Carpet' that night. It was a total write-off. But Fenton and the sister scrambled out without a scratch — another miracle. That was VH-UJN that was.

Dr Fenton crashing another aeroplane, although not exactly regarded as a routine exercise, was not unexpected. Anyway IOU, still in the Qantas hangar, was in perfect working order. It was held as security for 'Magic Carpet', but with people getting mangled up all over the place there wasn't much they could do and I suspect that they (whoever 'they' were) had pretty well thrown in the towel. Fenton went to Darwin by train and came back by air. A man had shot himself and the doctor had to go and make sure he was dead. He needn't have worried really. When he got to the place the body had already been buried. 'But,' Fenton protested, 'You can't do that without a doctor's certificate.' 'We had to,' he was told. 'He smelt too much.'

Then came a devastating blow. A cable arrived from Swatow in China announcing that his sister, who was married to a Dutch diplomat, had died. His mother, who had gone up some weeks previously on a visit, was in shock from the terrible blow. Fenton's decision was instantaneous, he would fly to China.

It didn't take long for the news to reach DCA, which sent him a lengthy telegram, the gist of which was that a permit to leave the country would not be issued until his machine had passed an exhaustive airworthiness test for an overseas flight. And furthermore, he would have to produce the clearances and permits necessary to land and fly over foreign countries, all of which would take if not months then certainly weeks. It seemed like he'd have to put in a few short cuts.

From Darwin it was approximately 550 miles across the Timor Sea to his first landfall but there was an emergency airstrip and fuel supply at Cape Four-croy on Bathurst Island. Landing there and topping up his tank would reduce the lonely flight by seventy miles, but that would not be enough.

His previous aeroplane, the 'Magic Carpet', was still resting peacefully at Munbulloo. With the help of a plumber he recovered the battered fuel tank, installed it in the passenger cockpit and put together an ingenious and desperate medley of pipes and pumps to transfer fuel to the main tank situated on, and part of, the upper wing. Then he took off for Bathurst Island from where, after hastily topping up his tank, he flew into the vast void of the Arafura Sea.

It was the first week in March and the wet season was by no means spent. It usually wound up with savage cyclonic storms which could cover a very wide area and towered thousands of feet above, split with savage lightning which can easily engulf a tiny aeroplane like the Moth and spit out the pieces. He flew through such a storm and it was only by the grace of God and good luck that he came out the other side in one piece.

The Island, then known as Timor and under Dutch dominion, came into sight late in the afternoon. Wondering what sort of reception he would get without any proper clearances or papers, Fenton landed wearily at Koepang. He gratefully received VIP treatment. From there he crossed another two hundred and fifty miles of turbulent sea, interspersed with monsoonal storms, refuelled without incident at Rambang, then flew on to Sourabaya where some necessary maintenance work was done without any problems.

He struck his first snag at Singapore. His intentions were to leave at midnight, and his old friend the moon was beaming down with an unusual brilliance. The Royal Air Force, however, told him that he would not be allowed to leave unless a flare path was laid down, for which they required a cheque. Bad luck, no cheque book, he explained. The heavily braided Royal Air Force gentleman became extremely acrimonious. No cheque — then no flare path. No flare path — no go.

As could be expected, the doctor won in the end. They finally relented and a quarter of a mile of fifty-watt bulbs blazed along each side of the runway as he prepared for take-off at midnight. A young officer told to supervise his departure listened with a straight face as Fenton shook hands with him and assured him that if the Royal Air Force ever came to Katherine they could use his flare path for free.

Penang was next, then Bangkok, where he got his first good night's rest — twelve hours straight. From there Fenton flew across Thailand, then called Siam, landing at an obscure aerodrome, Nakon Panom, where some language and other difficulties were sorted out by the timely arrival of a Siamese doctor to whom he made himself understood in halting French. Leaving Nakon Panom he set a course for Hanoi but weather compelled him to make an emergency landing on a beach, with a fuel gauge showing a severely reduced set of tanks.

After an uncomfortable night he made an early start for Fort Bayard hoping to refuel, but found the aerodrome blanketed in fog and had to return to his beach until it cleared. After getting his tanks refilled he flew to Hong Kong where his arrival was anticipated. The British Consul had sent a cable advising that he would certainly end up in jail if he didn't have all the necessary clearances and permits. This was further compounded by the Aerodrome Controller demanding his pilot's licence and Certificate of Airworthiness, both of which had been withheld by the Australian authorities. He was informed that he was grounded. So far the flying doctor had had to talk his way through Dutch, Siamese and French territory. It was infuriating to find himself blocked by the British.

Swatow, his destination, was only two and a half hours flying from Hong Kong. He argued and pleaded for nearly an hour, eventually wearing down their resistance and agreeing to sign a document of considerable length which he didn't even attempt to read. He left at four o'clock in the afternoon, landed at Swatow just before sundown, put his aeroplane in a hangar — and was promptly arrested.

Treated with traditional Chinese courtesy and liberally plied with endless cups of China tea, Fenton was held in custody until the arrival of an officer, Colonel Woon, who had spent some years in America and spoke fluent English. The Colonel was followed by the British Consul, who severely reprimanded the Australian pilot even though the situation was explained to him. Neither Fenton's brother-in-law, who was the Dutch Consul, nor Clyde's mother were aware of his arrival. He believed that to have let his mother know he was flying to China would only have added to her distress.

After a week's rest, Fenton arranged his mother's passage back to Australia by ship and set off for home himself. Inevitably, there was again friction in Hong Kong where he was told he was grounded until his aeroplane was given a thorough airworthiness check, which could take weeks. The Governor, although sympathetic, refused to intervene and, to make matters worse, Cook, back in Darwin, had arranged for him to attend a malarial course in Singapore. So, Fenton arranged for the Shell agent to refuel the aeroplane, obtained permission to check it, started the motor on the pretence of testing a magneto — and took off before their eyes!!

Heading for Fort Bayard, his guardian angel, without so much as a by-your-leave deserted him. Pressure of business perhaps. The engine developed a frightening vibration and Fenton had to make a forced landing on a beach, coming to rest with half the plane in the sea. Fortunately a group of friendly fishermen hauled him from the water. His guardian angel had returned, one hopes with appropriate apologies, and he was able to rectify the trouble and get into the air once more. Via Fort Bayard, Torene, Saigon, Kampong Trach and Penang he reached Singapore, completed the malarial course, and once again faced the long, lonely flight across the Arafura Sea.

And so this remarkably modest man returned to Darwin, as nonchalantly as he had left. He had completed a flight of more than nine thousand miles over lonely stretches of turbulent ocean, over hundreds of miles of hungry mountains reaching up to claw him down and through raging storms of unbelievable ferocity in a flimsy single-engine wood and fabric Tiger Moth, with hardly any preparation and almost every man's hand turned against him.

It was an epic flight worthy of international recognition, but apart from an enthusiastic welcome from close friends who had gathered at the Fanny Bay Aerodrome to watch for his return, the only official attention Fenton received was from his old friends, the Department of Uncivil Aviation, who predictably grounded him.

Equally predictably that didn't last long. A little Aboriginal boy at Dunmara Station three or four hundred miles to the south, had been badly injured by a buffalo bull. The men were away mustering and the buffalo had taken charge of the only waterhole. 'Please bring a rifle,' he was asked. He flew off to the lonely cattle station, shot the buffalo and brought the child and its mother back to Darwin hospital. Sadly though, the injuries were massive and the child died.

Then Bathurst Island was hit with a serious 'flu epidemic and a call for medical supplies reached the Flying Doctor who immediately prepared for a flight across the Straight to the Mission Station. He took a friend along for the ride. Whatever went wrong was never explained. Perhaps, after all its travels and travail, IOU just gave up the ghost. Taking off from the Fanny Bay airstrip, the aircraft tried hard enough but could not quite clear the trees at the end of the runway. It crashed and burst into flames. That was the end of IOU.

This time it was close — very, very close. The passenger escaped but the doctor was badly battered and burned about the face. Cook insisted that he go to hospital and get himself repaired, to which Fenton very reluctantly agreed. He was very depressed, having no aeroplane and no money to buy another one.

When this became known across the country the response was immediate. Never was a subscription filled so quickly, and once again Qantas came up with a Gyspy Moth which, after a turbulent career in Canada as a seaplane, had eventually found its way to Australia. It had been completely rebuilt and had a few additional refinements. At a ceremony on the Fanny Bay aerodrome it was christened 'Robin' after Dr Cook's daughter. Once again the Flying Doctor was in the air.

I had come in to Darwin from my buffalo hunting camp and at my first stop, the Victoria Hotel, I felt the air of gloom when I walked into the bar.

'What's wrong with this bloody place?' I asked the barman.

'Fenton's been missing for two days.'

'Christ! Don't tell me! Whereabouts?'

'Somewhere between Newcastle Waters and Boroolooloo.'

'Jesus!' I said 'That's a lot of country.'

'About a hundred thousand square miles,' he agreed gloomily.

The man next to me said, 'He's been pushing his luck for a long time.' It was a statement I had to agree with.

The following day there was still no news. Five or six aeroplanes, including an Air Force Dragon Rapide, were searching. There was still no sign on the fourth day. Fenton must have gone down in the sea, we thought. I had delivered a load of buffalo hides and bought salt and other supplies, and normally would have been on my way back well before this. But I hated to leave without any news of him, good or bad.

I tried to visualise a Northern Territory without Clyde Fenton and couldn't. Up to now he'd never been lost — not really lost. After all, he was constantly flying over miles of country with only six townships, five of them strung along the Overland Telegraph line, and not an inch of bitumen road anywhere, not even in Darwin.

On September 20th, 1937 Fenton had flown to Beetaloo Station to attend to a maternity case and then returned to Newcastle Waters to refuel, landing by the light of a full moon. He took off at sunrise the following morning, intending to do a circuit of several stations starting with the peculiarly named O.T. Station. There was a strong south-easter blowing when he took off which increased in intensity to almost gale strength. The country was flat and featureless apart from a network of creeks and watercourses which he had difficulty fitting to his chart. Homesteads were any- thing from fifty to a hundred miles apart in that spar- sely settled country. He knew that the O.T. Station was

Ground sign that led to Dr Fenton's rescue.

a group of bark bush buildings which would comfortably merge into the surrounding landscape.

After four hours of frustrated cruising his petrol gauge was getting ominously low. Half an hour later he knew that he would have to land and he had been looking for a suitable clearing. He knew that the alarm would be sounded the following morning but it still might be days before he was found. Therefore the essential thing was water. He could go a long time without food but would only last hours without water in that climate.

Eventually, Fenton spied a fairly large waterhole with a clear black soil plain nearby and, after circling a couple of times for a good look, made a safe landing. It was a very desolate spot but reasonably open, and the plane would be clearly visible from the air. In a couple of days at the outside, he thought, he'd be rescued. It was Tuesday September 21st. A quick look at his supplies disclosed a handful of malted milk tablets and a small bottle of brandy — the pluses were a bit on the short side and there were plenty of minuses.

Fenton's first task was to do something that would assist his rescuers to find him. Selecting the most suitable area for landing he pegged it, cutting stakes and tying a length of bandage on each. The flies were in their millions and never let up until sunset, when the mosquitoes took over. He had no bedding, but collected some dried grass and, with surgical gown, some towels and a sheet used in maternity cases, put a makeshift bed together. Daylight came and he walked back to the waterhole for a swim and saw a cow inextricably bogged. Meat! Food! When he approached it, however, the animal proved very active, bellowing and waving its head angrily. If he was going to get a feed of meat he'd have to kill it — but how? He was very inexperienced in such things, and retreated to think. Next day he stunned the cow with a hammer from his tool kit and with his pocket knife cut its throat.

Fenton hacked off a quantity of meat, took it to his camp and cooked some on the open fire. Tough and tasteless, but sustenance nevertheless. By Friday, though, all his meat supply had gone bad. On Saturday he tried fishing, using silk sutures for a line and a crude hook fashioned from split pins. The fish just laughed. On Sunday the stench from the dead cow was unbearable. He tried to shoot a duck with the Very pistol but the recoil split his nose, which streamed blood, and almost stunned him. It gave him an awful headache too. The flies attacked his split nose in a frenzy. On Monday, thoroughly dejected, his nose painful and bleeding intermittently, he was at his lowest ebb. The dead cow had attracted a pack of dingoes whose mournful howling further added to his misery.

On Tuesday morning Fenton awoke in a state of utter dejection, sure that he would die of starvation and the dingoes would tear his body to pieces as they were doing to the dead cow. Sitting under the wing of his aeroplane cursing the flies, the pangs of hunger almost unendurable, he heard a faint hum. Gradually it increased in volume and soon he saw the plane — but would it see him? Suddenly it banked steeply and flew straight towards him, circling a couple of times then coming in low for a bumpy landing. Flight Lt. Healy climbed from the plane followed by his crew. It was a joyful reunion.

Dr Cook ordered Fenton to take some leave. At the same time the Federal Government suddenly came good with a promise it had been chewing over for years. A telegram to Cook advised him that a brand new Fox Moth, a cabin plane fitted with a stretcher and accommodation for a nurse, was at de Havilands ready to fly.

Soon afterwards while flying his new plane, half way between Darwin and Katherine at an altitude of three thousand feet, Fenton was startled by a movement at his feet. Looking down, he saw the head of a brown snake, undoubtedly one of the most deadly in the world. In a state of mortal terror he landed, got the terrified sister out and killed the snake. Life for the flying doctor was rarely dull.

In 1941 Fenton joined the Air Force, not in his capacity as a doctor, but as a pilot. Initially he was a flying instructor, but that did not last long. Because of his unparalleled knowledge of the Territory, Northern Command soon had him transferred to the area he knew and loved so well. With the rank of Squadron Leader he was given a fleet of obsolete aircraft with a base at Batchelor, south of Darwin — a squadron which rapidly achieved notoriety as Fenton's Flying Freighters. It was mainly search and rescue work with aeroplanes that no one else wanted, which, although obsolete, could land on a pocket handkerchief. One of his pilots, Flight Lieutenant Tom French, wrote in a letter to me:

'I was fortunate enough to serve under Doc

Fenton as he was known to everyone. I had
quite a few postings in the RAAF but they were
dim memories compared with my happy life
with the "Doc"...

Doc's unit belied his reputation for hare-
brained risk-taking and he was a lovable
disciplinarian, which sounds a somewhat
strange mixture. Fenton's Flying Freighters
were talked of in every RAAF camp in
Australia.'

After the war he had a short stint with the Northern
Territory Medical Service before being appointed
Assistant Medical Officer for the State of Victoria. He
married a very lovely lady, Bon Catalano, the widow of
a colleague who was killed in a car accident.

Clyde Fenton passed away on February 28th, 1982.

DROVERS, DROUGHTS
AND DRY STAGES

TO THE AVERAGE traveller the cattle country of the
North, from the Kimberleys of Western Australia,
across the Northern Territory to the Gulf country, may
not have advanced much in recent years. Homesteads
are anything up to fifty miles apart, they are still
isolated by floodwaters, their stock are still decimated
by drought and flood and the flies and mosquitoes still
arrive in their teeming millions right on time.

But the people who live there, in spite of inconven-
iences imposed by nature, have luxuries that were
undreamed of. They are nurtured by air travel, televi-
sion, refrigerators, reliable means of transport and, if
they so desire, they can pick up a telephone and ring
New York or London. Their stock, in many cases, are
mustered by helicopter and whisked away to market in
road trains without losing condition.

It was not so very long ago when cattle walked
distances of up to a thousand miles at the dazzling
speed of ten miles a day over stock routes that were

126

frequently bare, going for days on end without water and arriving at their destination emaciated skeletons. Some of the distances travelled without water were incredible. Two brothers, Harry and Hugh Farquarson, took a thousand bullocks from Mistake Creek Station on the border of Western Australia to Queensland, a journey of nearly a thousand miles. One drive from Top Spring on the Armstrong River to Newcastle Waters was a hundred and ten miles and the few waterholes over that stretch, Marranji, Yellow Waterhole, The Bucket had barely enough water for their horses — so the bullocks had to go without. They got every beast to water without losing one which was an epic feat.

Jack Clark, a Boulia drover, was not so fortunate. He took delivery of five hundred bullocks from Glengyle Station, one of Sir Sidney Kidman's properties, with their destination Farina, the railhead. Two stock route bores were broken down and there was a ninety mile dry stage. Over this stretch they travelled mostly at night. Apart from the advantage of it being much cooler there was a good moon. On the night before they would have got to water the cattle walked until about three a.m., the moon had set and so the cattle were rested until day broke.

Although the bullocks were dangerously thirsty they would have got to water by about ten or eleven the next morning. But during the early hours of the morning a sandstorm of unusual intensity built up. The sandstorms in that area have to be experienced to be believed. This one blinded the men on watch so it was impossible to see the cattle. There was no way they could hold them, it was a blinding impossibility. The drovers lost control and the cattle, almost dying of thirst walked in the only direction they knew there was water — back the way they had come. When daylight broke there were no cattle. They were gone. Clark's horses were too thirsty to follow them and he had to get them to water. Every bullock died.

Sturts Creek is one of Australia's inland waterways that never reach the sea. It heads on Inverway Station in the Northern Territory, winds its way in a south-westerly direction, crosses the West Australian border, turns south and finally floods out into Lake Billaluna. Billaluna Station covers about a thousand square miles of the surrounding country and is probably the most isolated property in the whole of Australia. Because of its isolation, its marketing problem was worse than most. In its earliest days there was no meatworks at Wyndham but there was a market at Wiluna in the goldfields, with an eight hundred mile stretch without water.

Eventually this difficulty was overcome. The West Australian Government engaged a surveyor named Canning who first mapped the track with eight men and ten camels. It was established that water was obtainable at fairly shallow depths and so wells were put down and equipped with windlass, bucket and an arrangement known as a whip. The Canning Stock Route was open.

Billaluna Station was ready to take advantage of the new track and had a droving plant standing owned by two partners, Thompson and Shoesmith. They were to have the honour of taking the first mob of bullocks down the Canning Stock Route. Not very far behind them would be another drover, Tom Cole, a namesake of mine but in no way related. He had recently married Mabel Bridge, the daughter of the owner of Mabel Downs. Joe Bridge had named the station after his daughter and when she married Tom Cole, Bridge gave the young couple five hundred bullocks for a wedding present.

The bridegroom wasted no time. He got his young wife pregnant and headed for the Canning Stock Route to take advantage of the shortage of cattle at the goldmining town of Wiluna at the other end. He was two weeks behind Thompson and Shoesmith. In many respects it was not a difficult trip for experienced drovers although there was very little surface water.

In a letter to me, a younger son, Sandy Cole, told the dramatic story:

> My grandfather, Joe Bridge, owned Mabel Downs Station. Joe Bridge gave Dad five hundred bullocks for a wedding present so he thought he would take them through to Wiluna. He put a plant of horses together and took his brother, or maybe two brothers, two black fellows, a cook named Jack the Rager (a man with that name would have to be a cook) and another bloke and a policeman called Pennefather. (I have not been able to ascertain whether Pennefather went in an official capacity or what) and two blue heeler cattle dogs that saved his life on more than one occasion.

He then describes the country and goes on to say how his father discovered Thompson and Shoesmith's remains:

> Dad buried Thompson and Shoesmith and a yellow fellow, three black fellows and a white fellow. He made camp there [at a place that became know as the Haunting Well] for one week and put fences round their graves. He said they had been dead about a fortnight. The stock perished and the blacks ate the tucker and cut up all the saddles.

His letter continues:

> They tried to work out how to shoot with the guns but by the evidence, they shot one of their own, fortunately

for Dad that happened. Dad said Shoesmith and Thompson made one error that cost them their lives, by letting the gins into the camp and the blacks speared them all.

Dad told me he never allowed them into the camp, never shot a gin or piccaninny but the bucks he came in touch with died of lead poisoning [they were shot]. It was a battle of tactics, who got who first.

Eventually Dad got through. Tom Cole, my eldest brother, was born while Dad was taking the cattle through. [There were three Tom Coles in Northern Australia back then, Sandy Cole's father, his eldest brother and myself. I was known as Tom Cole the breaker.]

Dad bought a pub at Day Dawn near Coolgardie but never did any good. He came back and took up land near Bedford Downs called Corola Valley. I was born there. Dad brought me into the world. I was a fortnight old when I got into Halls Creek.

The giant multinational company, Vestey's, have now divested themselves of most of their cattle stations, but just before World War I, with remarkable foresight, the company began a tremendous operation buying huge areas from the Kimberleys to Queensland. There were seventeen properties totalling between thirty and forty thousand square miles and a meatworks was built in Darwin.

At the outbreak of the World War I the cattle stations they had acquired were producing twenty thousand bullocks a year which were processed in their meatworks. The Blue Star Line, which they also owned, took the finished product to England. Their enormous contribution to the war effort was exceeded only by the massive profits on which, we have recently been given to understand, by a brilliant form of accounting they have been able to avoid any demands from the taxation authorities.

The meatworks had a short and turbulent career with industrial troubles and the end of World War I contributed to its decease. This entailed a readjustment and the cattle that wended their way northward had to turn to the east. The company owned stations in Queensland and also meatworks in Townsville but it was a long dreary journey with one stretch of two hundred and eighty miles and one waterhole.

The Federal Government reluctantly came to the rescue, after all the Northern Territory was its baby, albeit an illegitimate one, with no sire to represent it in parliament. The governors of our country no doubt frequently wished that it had been stillborn but every now and then it gave a lusty squawk, which gave rise to feelings of unease in the corridors of power from time to time. An Administrator had recently been put on a boat and packed off with instructions to get out and stay out. So, the Federal Government must have thought, if the bastards want water for God's sake let's give it to them and shut them up.

A Mr Peacock was engaged to put bores down across the Barcly Tablelands through the Murranji track. He was a man of deep religious convictions which he was able to subdue when it came to the pursuit of his chosen vocation. It was found later that he had struck water at around the two to three hundred foot level in most of the holes, but he pushed his drills down a further two hundred feet. This, at the worst, could only be regarded as a minor peccadillo. He was paid five shillings a foot.

The bores were fitted with windmills thirty feet across, on steel framed towers sixty feet in height, which pumped water into huge earthen tanks. And so the cattle that walked from Western Australia to

Queensland could get a drink every thirty miles. By now twenty thousand bullocks in mobs of twelve hundred and fifty, travelling a few days apart, walked to Queensland.

The men who overlanded the cattle were a breed of their own and rightly hold a special place in the history of the outback. A drover's plant, as it was always known, consisted of forty to fifty horses, sometimes more. Eight or ten would be pack horses, six or eight were night horses that were used exclusively for watching the cattle at night — very special horses indeed, surefooted with flawless eyesight they were used for nothing else. The rest were stock horses with each man allocated three saddle horses which he rode in turn so that each horse had two days' spell. On the long trips a mob of bullocks was from a thousand to thirteen hundred and this usually took seven or eight men, including the boss drover and a cook.

One man was the horse tailer, a very important job. He was in complete charge of the horses and saw that they were watered and that they were hobbled out on the best grass be could find, which sometimes involved opening the odd fence. He did the first watch and was called at the same time as the cook, usually about four a.m., to the resounding cry of 'daylight'. There wasn't a glimmer of course, it was pitch dark, but he would take the spare night horse and ride out and find the particular horses due for work that day. Not as easy as it sounds for although bells were on the horses required by early morning they were hell west and crooked, perhaps a couple of miles from the first to the last. But a good horse tailer would have them at the camp before the men had finished their breakfast, then he would snatch his meal, muster the rest, help the cook to pack up, throw packs on and off to the next camp. On the plains he would have to find firewood and that would go on a pack horse too. If there was no firewood, and frequently there wasn't, then he would have to rustle up enough dung for the cook to boil the billy. It wasn't always enough to boil the water but, as a cook would sometimes say, 'It's as hot as they can bloody well drink it'. On a dry stage water was carried in canteens, not enough for six or eight to wash in but enough for a drink and the cooking.

The one thing dreaded by drovers was what, in their vernacular, is termed a 'rush' — a stampede at night. The cattle were rounded up on camp at night and they peacefully lay down and chewed the cud, slept, stood up sometimes for a stretch and lay down again, and then, in one split second, they were all on their feet galloping. It was an awe-inspiring experience. A thousand bullocks on their feet and galloping sounds like rolling thunder and never failed to evoke 'the butterflies' in the most experienced drover. As one put it to me once, 'My bowels turn to porridge'.

For a moment, the man on watch tightened his grip on the reins, his horse, probably a veteran of many stampedes before, is fighting for the bit, a good horse knows his work. It took a moment to determine the direction the mob took, but only a moment, and then the horseman let the horse have its head and in great sweeping strides he raced for the lead. He had to get up to the leaders and turn them. By this time another man had leapt into the saddle of the spare night horse and was backing him up on the wing. Swinging their stock whips, they gradually turned the leaders into the tail and soon they were rung up. It took some time for them to settle down — no more sleep that night. When daylight broke the mob were counted. It would have been unusual if there were not a few missing, if so a man was told off to track them up. He may have found them soon enough to rejoin the mob the same day, but not always.

And so they rode day after day, finding grass and water for the cattle and horses. Rolling their swags out on the ground, watching the cattle at night, a hasty breakfast in the dark and, for the midday meal, a hunk of corned meat and damper and perhaps a quartpot of tea and supper in the dark again.

On long trips the flour became infested with weevils and the corned beef a haven for dung beetles. If there was water to spare they could be removed by soaking it in water and skimming most of them off. A dedicated cook would remove most of them if they were camped close enough to water, but few of them were that dedicated.

Sixteen hours was an average day in a droving camp, for which the men were paid five pounds a week, a cook commanding six. 'More than those bastards are worth', could be sometimes heard, although not in their hearing.

My own droving experiences have been varied and some of them I have recounted in *Hell West & Crooked.* The only one of which I have a record was when I took seventeen hundred head of cattle, together with eight horses, twelve packs and a waggonette for carrying supplies, on to a thousand square miles of land, a distance of nearly four hundred miles.

It all started when I saw an advertisement in the *Government Gazette* for several blocks of land with areas varying from six hundred square miles to fifteen hundred. I put in an application for the medium-sized thousand square mile block and, being the only applicant, was successful. It was on the Barkly Tablelands, Mitchell and Flinders grass downs which presented a much more attractive proposition than my own property, Esmeralda Station, which was rough and scrubby with wild cattle which involved a lot of hard galloping.

The downs country was much better quality grass and closer to markets so there were several advantages, including the production of fatter and better cattle. However, to muster my herd and move them down was a very big undertaking. Consequently I invited a cattleman friend to join me, to which he readily agreed. His country too could, at the best, only be described as rough breeding country. Our combined herds, as I have explained, totalled seventeen hundred and, of course, because we were going on to an unoccupied block of country we needed a lot of working horses, equipment and, stores being few and far between, enough rations to feed ten or twelve stockmen.

My property, Esmeralda Station, was about fifteen hundred square miles of rugged country and because it was well watered the cattle were not only scattered hell west and crooked but wild as March hares as well, involving a lot of hard riding to muster them up. I had a good head stockman, a halfcaste who had been with me for many years, a top bushman and a slashing horseman. The rest of my team were Aboriginal stockmen, most of whom had been with me in my buffalo hunting camp. Having come to an agreement with my cattleman friend, Jack Guild, the arrangement was that I would muster my herd and bring them to his property, which was about a hundred and fifty miles south on the way to the new block on the Barkly Tablelands.

The mustering of my cattle turned out to be a much tougher proposition than I anticipated as the wet season took up later than usual. Eventually I got them together and, after going through the formalities of making out waybills, together with my stock boys I set off for Guild's property with eight hundred head of cattle.

The first night or two was hard riding keeping the cattle together but I picked a full moon to start, knowing that for the first few nights the cattle would be restless, which is normal. After a couple of nights they settle down and get used to being rounded up after sundown, usually giving no trouble. One stockman could hold them easily. So far it was a very straightforward operation and it took a couple of weeks to reach Jack Guild's place. Jack's cattle were in hand which, with my herd, made up to seventeen hundred. The next two or three days were very busy stocking up with rations and, on Friday March 13th, I set off.

My diary records:

> W. Moore started at £7 a week [a good wage in those days] and keep. We left with 1700 head of mixed cattle, 81 plant horses and 12 packs. W. Moore in charge of cattle and seven boys [Aboriginal stockman] Travelled three miles and camped.

All my diary entries were necessarily brief and, although not mentioned, I also had a waggonette which carried surplus rations. There were no stores along the stock route and there were nine hungry mouths to feed.

It must be understood that the cattle had to be watched at night and for the first two or three days didn't take to it too kindly. In fact they surged all night trying to get away. It took several nights to settle them down, taking three men at a time to hold them but once they settled down and got used to being watched one man could hold them on camp easily.

The horses, of course, had to be hobbled out on the best feed we could find. This wasn't a problem as soon after the wet season there was a lush growth of grass everywhere. Mustering the horses up in the morning was a different proposition. Even though they were hobbled they could walk a long way in a night. It is easy to believe that eighty horses can get quite a scatter on in a night. My diary says on Saturday March 14th:

> Five horses away this morning. Sent one boy after them (to track them up). Packed up and went on to Yellow Hole. Boy returned with only two horses. Too late to send back for the others and too shorthanded.

The next day, Sunday 15th:

> Some cattle got away last night. Billy Moore tracked them up and got them. Went on to the Stirling River.

By this time the cattle had settled down and I reached the boundary of Elsey Station made famous by Mrs Aneas Gunn in her classic *We of The Never Never*. Mark O'Conner, the Elsey head stockman, joined us here to 'see us through the run'. I had already given them notice of my approach, which was compulsory mainly to keep drovers honest. It was by no means unknown for a drover to kill a beast belonging to the station he was passing through. Most drovers figured, 'They won't miss one.' There wouldn't be many stations the size of Elsey whose herd wasn't much under twenty-five thousand head.

From here, although the wet season was only just over, I knew that I was going to have problems with water as there were some long dry stretches in front of me. The Warlock was a large waterhole which never went dry and so my cattle and horses got their fill. But from here was a string of bores with windmills and although they were equipped with huge twenty-five thousand gallon tanks the tanks were rarely full because of the demands made on them by travelling stock. I had heard over the grapevine that there were at least two mobs of bullocks on the road which would seriously deplete them. I had to hope that the wind blew hard and steady for the next few days. Somewhere travelling north with bullocks were two drovers and I knew that they would drain the tanks.

ON SUNDAY 22ND my diary says:

> Watered cattle and horses (at the Warlock) and went out about four miles and camped. Twenty five miles to No. 1 bore, (the next water).

> MONDAY 23RD

> Got a good start this morning but buggy wheel broke. Lost three hours repairing it. Sent the night horses (the horses used for watching the cattle) and tomorrow's day horses back to Warlock for water. Caught cattle on dinner camp. Grant and Stacey with bullocks travelling north. Took plant (the horses) on to No. 1 bore and watered at 7 o'clock. Packed up two canteen horses with sixteen gallons of water and went back to the cattle, ten o'clock.

> TUESDAY 24TH

> Reached the cattle camp at 2 o'clock this morning. Got an hours sleep and started them (the cattle) off. Watered the buggy horses (from the canteens). Went on to the bore for another load of water and back to cattle. Camped four miles out (from the bore). Should make water about nine o'clock or ten o'clock tomorrow morning. Cattle very thirsty.

> WEDNESDAY 25TH

> Got the lead of the cattle to the bore at 8.30 this morning. Tank went dry after watering one

APRIL 1942

1 April WEDNESDAY 91-274

All the boys ran away about 12.30 this morning. Let the cattle go in the second wetil. Jack Guild, Moore & Calf mustering all night. Got nearly all of them by daylight. Rode into Birdum to try & get men. Engaged two half castes & several boys, to be at camp tomorrow.

2 THURSDAY 92-273

One half caste turned up this morning, the rest jibbed on it. Back to Birdum again. Got a promise from three boys

Entries from Tom Cole's diaries.

thousand two hundred head. Five hundred
head still to be watered. The next water is 14
miles, so position is serious. Camped them in the
heat of the day. Sent Moore on with the dry
mob. Packed up and brought the plant (horses,
packs and waggonette) and the rest of the
cattle. Caught up with Moore five miles out.

THURSDAY 26TH
Pushed the cattle off before daybreak. Sent one
boy back for them and took the droving plant
on. Cattle got a suck at a small waterhole. Mad
with thirst. Pushed them on to another larger
hole and got them half a drink of muddy water.
Got them another drink at sundown and
camped.

FRIDAY 27TH
Gave the cattle a days spell.

The next six days were uneventful, there was grass and
water in abundance. Then on April 1st (April Fools
Day!) all my stock boys ran away in the middle of the
night. By a stroke of good fortune Jack Guild was with
me having caught me up the day before. I suppose I
should have expected it. They were getting further and
further from their own country where all sorts of devil
devils abounded.

Although there were three of us mustering up
seventeen hundred head of cattle that had walked off
camp in the middle of the night it presented an enormous job getting them together again. Fortunately
they had kept together; at this time they were used to
the day to day routine of droving and maybe thought
that it was all fairly normal. Also it was open country
and, more by great good fortune, we managed to get
them in hand.

I managed to get another team together and on April 3rd I was on my way again.

APRIL 3RD
Got away this morning with four boys and one halfcaste, George Cummins. Camped at Six Mile.

APRIL 4TH
Dry camp, four or five miles from Ironstone Bore. Althaus passed with six hundred bullocks.

APRIL 5TH
Ironstone Bore. Left two cows and two calves.

I remember this clearly. The two cows had calved and it was impossible for them to have travelled.

The next water was Rodericks Bore and it would take me the best part of three days to get there. It was a hard three days. The horses were the most important. They had to be taken back to water as the cattle plodded over the dry stages day after day. I left Ironstone Bore on Monday and dry camped. The next day the horses were taken back for a drink. The next day I walked the cattle mostly at night and, as we got closer to the next water, Rodericks Bore, the horses were taken on. We reached the bore with the cattle on the morning of the third day.

The next three days were without incident. April 13th. I had been a month on the road and I noted: 'Good camp, plenty of water.' The 14th and 15th were uneventful. On the 16th I had to dry camp and the next day reached Dunmara, a good camp with feed and water plentiful. I was getting close to my destination. Dunmara was a roadside hotel owned by Noel Healey. I gave the cattle three days' spell and on the 21st I left Dunmara and dry camped. The next water was Frews Ponds where there was a good waterhole. My next stage was a comfortable day of nine miles to No. 7 Bore.

The weather turned intensely hot as I was faced with a long stretch over the Sturt Plain with not a single shade tree. From No. 7 bore I went out about five miles and camped. The next day I had a hard twenty miles to go and it turned out to be the hardest stretch of the entire trip. The cattle moved off just before the first crack of dawn and when the sun rose like a molten ball of fire the temperature quickly built up. There wasn't a skerrick of shade but before midday I had to round them up, if only to rest them in the searing heat. I held them until the fire was out of the sun. It is the only entry in my diary that makes any reference to the heat:

SUNDAY 20TH
Very hot day. Eight head of cattle perished crossing the Sturt Plain. Dropped others.

Another dry camp and I got them to water the following day. From here it was eight easy days following Newcastle Creek nearly all the way with plenty of grass and water. It was May 5th, seventy-three days since I left Esmeralda. Not that long in terms of droving but without a doubt the hardest seventy three days I've ever experienced — the number of cattle and horses, the worrying dry stages, rarely a proper night's sleep, filthy, unwashed and thirsty and shorthanded most of the time.

The relief was tremendous when I turned them out on to a plain stretching as far as the eye could see of beautiful waving Mitchell and Flinders grass. I thought of Banjo Patterson's immortal lines:

For a drover's life has pleasures
That the townsfolk never know.

Well, Banjo never went droving, that's for sure.

THE
TRIANGLE

I HAVE GIVEN a lot of thought as to whether I should tell
this story, but it happened a very long time ago and the
people concerned have long since crossed the Great
Divide. Because of the nature of the story it is still
clearly imprinted on my memory. Triangle Station
doesn't exist any more, not under that name. Over the
years it has changed hands many times, been broken
up and absorbed into other properties. For obvious
reasons I have changed the names of the people concerned. Just the same, for more than one reason I do
not want to be too exact about the locality.

I had been horsebreaking for Vesteys', the multinational cattle company which among other things, had
seventeen or eighteen cattle stations across the country from Queensland to Western Australia. They had a
few other odds and ends too, like the Blue Star Line,
extensive property in South Africa and North and
South America, not forgetting numerous meatworks
scattered round the world. You could say that they

were a company of considerable substance.

I had been head stockman on Wave Hill Station, one of their bigger properties, but I had forsaken that to take on horsebreaking for the company. There were several reasons why I left the security of a permanent job with, no doubt, the near certainty of a management in the not too distant future. First, a horsebreaker was on a contract and therefore largely his own boss. Secondly, I had an affinity with horses and although it was a bit rough at times I was a good enough horseman to handle it and I liked the work. And last, but no means least, it was the best paid job on a station.

On today's standards wages were unbelievably low and the time I am talking about, the twenties, were the years of the worst depression the world had ever known. As an example, the biggest property in the world at that time, or any other, was Victoria River Downs, owned by the meat extract people, Bovril. The manager of the station at that time was Alf Martin and his salary was fourteen pounds a week, or about twenty-eight dollars. And when you consider that the property was somewhere in the vicinity (nobody would have known exactly) of twelve thousand square miles, bigger than Holland, and ran a hundred and seventy thousand head of cattle it makes the manager sound a bit underpaid.

The company supplied him and his family with housing and rations, a Chinese cook who was paid three pounds (six dollars) a week, two or three Aboriginal girls who did housework and were paid nothing, and a gardener, also on the free list. Although all station hands from the manager down were kept, it was by no means lavish. The manager naturally did better than most. Fortunately there was no shortage of beef.

So the attraction of becoming a station manager some time in the future was not very great. As a horsebreaker I could earn more than twice a manager's wages, although there was the disadvantage of it being seasonal and I had just got to the stage where it had cut out for the season and a long stretch of nothing was looming up. It was getting on towards the end of the year and I had broken in at seven of Vesteys' stations. Although there were other properties there were also other breakers, and, to put it in a nutshell, I was out of work.

Like nearly all station workers my transport was horses. I had two pack horses which carried all my worldly goods, consisting of a swag containing a couple of blankets, a mosquito net (most essential), a spare pair of riding trousers and a couple of shirts. There were of course, other items too, towels, shaving gear, a book or two and various odds and ends, frequently referred to in the vernacular of the bushman as 'my forty years' gathering'. In the packbags was a camp-oven, a set of billycans, a week or so's rations, shoeing gear, spare horseshoes, an axe for cutting ridgepoles when setting up camp and, of course, a rifle which ensured that I would never go hungry. There would be other odds and ends too numerous to mention, but all in all I was completely self-contained.

I had four good saddle horses which were ridden on alternate days because, it must be remembered, they lived on grass and sometimes grass was not always in plentiful supply. Horses like humans must eat and although at times, especially along stock routes where thousands of bullocks have travelled, it was scarce, a good horseman would find a feed for his horses somewhere. One frequently sees illustrations of what is supposed to be a stockman riding a horse and carrying a bundle on the pommel of his saddle, usually wrongly described as a 'bedroll'. No bushman ever called it anything else but a 'swag', and if he tried to put it on the saddle of his riding horse there would be no room for the horseman.

I was stocking up my packs at a bush store. The storekeeper, whom I knew quite well, asked me which way I was heading.

'I'm not sure,' I said, 'the breaking has cut out.'

'Well,' he said, 'if you're interested the Triangle is looking for a breaker, or was a week ago and I haven't heard of anyone taking it on.'

This was good news and I was pretty sure, the way news travels in that country, he would have heard had anyone turned up. The store was the centre of everything. I reckoned that it was about thirty miles to Triangle Station. This was confirmed by the storekeeper who said, 'You'll probably meet the mailman along the road, he's due back tomorrow.' I asked about water as it was getting dry and he said that there was only one waterhole, Pelican Hole, twenty-one miles out, which left nine miles to the property. I decided that I'd get an early start the next morning, twenty-one miles was a comfortable stage the first day and nine miles was a short lap the next.

I got away at sunrise and riding along the lonely road, my horses trotting along ahead of me, my thoughts turned to the station towards which I was heading. It was one of the few properties managed by the owner. Mostly they were either owned by big companies like Vesteys or some southern Pitt Street cattleman.

I tried to recall something of what I had heard of the place and the owner. Mark Ellison was different from the usual run-of-the-mill cattleman, which he hadn't always been. I knew that early on he had branched into mining, struck gold out in the desert, sold out to a mining company and bought the Triangle with the proceeds. There was also a story that he'd married a woman who was a good bit younger, an outstanding horsewoman.

The sun was straight overhead when I sighted a cluster of gums which I rightly took to be Pelican Hole, the water the storekeeper told me about. The last couple of hours had been hot and my horses trotted up and plunged their noses into the water and drank deeply. As they were taking their fill I caught sight of a wisp of smoke rising further up the creek and half a dozen packsaddles near by. I concluded it was the mailman the storekeeper had mentioned.

When my horses had taken their fill of water they walked up the bank and stood around waiting to be unpacked, knowing that it would be our night camp. I selected a spot further along, fifty yards or so from the mailman who walked over when he saw me and, with a friendly grin, extended a leathery hand saying, 'G'day stranger.'

'G'day,' I replied, 'Tom Cole's the name and where can I get a feed for my horses?'

He looked me up and down and said, 'You must be Tom Cole the breaker?'

I nodded and he went on, 'The only place you'll get any grass is across the creek. About half a mile over, you'll come to a fence. You'll have to open it at a strainer post.'

I thanked him, unpacked and took my horses in the direction he indicated. I picked up tracks which I rightly took to be the mailman's horses and soon came to a line of fence. Inside about twenty head of hobbled horses were feeding, the mailman's for sure. I had no trouble undoing the wires and when my horses walked through I hobbled them and hung my saddle and bridle up in the fork of a tree. I had seen dingo tracks and I didn't want my girths chewed by hungry wild dogs.

I walked back to my camp and was busy making a fire when the mailman walked over. I thanked him again for the information on the grass and remarked that it was surprising it hadn't been eaten out by drovers. I knew that a lot of cattle went through in the season. 'No way,' he said, 'they always put a stockman on to see them through. They don't mind me putting my horses in, it's not like a thousand head of hungry bullocks.' He added, 'A mailman always gets looked after anyway.' Which I knew to be right. He then said, looking at the billy I had put on the fire, 'Come over to my camp for a feed. I've got some good Triangle beef.' I gratefully accepted, not so much because of the fresh meat but because I wanted to hear something about the station I was heading for.

We sat on a log beside his fire and had a good bushman's meal washed down by billy tea. I let the mailman do the talking. Like most bushmen he was a good raconteur and he confirmed that Ellison wanted a breaker. I asked him what the horses were like.

'Not too bad, I'd say about general run-of-the-mill types. He's got a good stallion which is starting to show in the younger horses.' As he put another log on the fire, I steered the conversation to Ellison's mining.

'Didn't he shoot someone?' I asked.

The mailman laughed, 'Yes, I'm not sure of the full story. I don't think it was very serious, the bloke didn't die. It had something to do with claim jumping, but he was never charged with anything. They aren't too fussy in the Territory.'

I asked him how big the Triangle was and he said he thought that it was about a thousand square miles, 'give or take a couple of hundred.'

I said that I heard that the blacks were bad out the back of the run and he nodded.

'The place backs on to the ranges and there's a mob

of Myalls there who come down when they get hungry and spear cattle, but I think Ellison can handle them.' He went on to say, 'He's got a mad boundary rider you're bound to meet, a strange sort of bastard. Most boundary riders are, I s'pose, living out there on their own they get that way. He's always talking about what he dreams. He's s'posed to dream about what's going to happen. Some blokes swear by him, but I dunno. A strange sort of bastard', he repeated. 'Mrs Ellison works in the stock camp doesn't she? Good horsewoman I believe.' 'His wife? Yes, a top rider, terrible good looking too, a fair bit younger than Ellison I'd say, "Gypsy" he calls her.' I asked him how many breakers I'd get and he reckoned about twenty odd. About a month's work, I thought.

The next morning saw both of us packed by sunrise. We said brief goodbyes and whips cracked as we headed in opposite directions, he to the township to get ready for his next mail run and myself for the Triangle. It was mid-morning when I caught sight of roofs reflecting the sunlight and at the same time I came to a gate on which was nailed a crude notice, 'Triangle Station'. I opened the gate and my horses walked through.

A neat homestead sat on a ridge overlooking a lagoon. To the right was a group of buildings which I took to be a saddle room and equipment shed and probably men's quarters. A couple of hundred yards further over was a set of cattle yards from which a cloud of dust was rising. I could hear cattle bellowing. I left my packs and rode over towards the yard and sat on my horse watching cattle being drafted. There was one white man and several Aboriginal stockmen working them. They appeared to be drafting off weaners.

One of the stockboys saw me first and spoke to the white man who looked over and then climbed through the rails as I dismounted. We greeted one another and I said, 'I'm Tom Cole, I understand you wanted a breaker.' 'Yes, I certainly do and I'm very pleased to see you.' Standing about five foot ten, I guessed him to be about thirty-five, lean, wiry and sunburnt with stern features that broke up into a pleasant smile. 'Let your horses go and one of my boys will put them out in the big paddock as soon as I've finished with this lot,' he said nodding towards the cattle.

Half an hour later Ellison joined me as I was stacking my gear away and he got straight down to business.

'I'm not sure how many breakers there are. Between twenty and twenty-five. There are a few three year olds that are probably forward enough to throw a rope on, we'll see. They're running away at the back of the run. We'll start mustering them tomorrow or the next day. I've got some book work to tidy up first. Hate bloody book work.' He showed me where the breaking tackle was kept and went to the house.

At sundown I made my way to the kitchen. A very large Aboriginal woman was sweating over a hot stove where huge steaks were sizzling. A young Aboriginal girl, sitting on the floor at the back, kept the punkah swinging with a cord tied to her big toe — a surprisingly effective cooling system.

The next morning, after an early breakfast, I went to the saddle room and laid out the breaking tackle, headstalls and greenhide ropes. Everything was in good condition, obviously looked after. There were three sets. A young woman walked up and said, 'I'm Mrs Ellison, I s'pose you're Tom Cole.' She put her hand out quite naturally and I took it nervously. I wasn't used to managers' or owners' wives shaking hands, or even passing the time of day. Actually managers' wives were quite rare in that country and owners' wives even rarer, and as for them talking to a horsebreaker...

I was getting my breath back from the encounter when she said, 'I think we'll be starting the horse muster today.' I nodded, watching her as she walked over to the saddle rail and examined a saddle. I remembered what the mailman had said, that she was 'terrible good looking' and thought that it wasn't exactly the description I would have applied to her. I thought that she was one of the most beautiful women I had ever seen. The few managers' wives I'd seen from a distance were usually two or three axe handles wide with faces like a mallee root and twice as tough.

Her hair was jet black and tied back and she had dark vibrant eyes. With her jodhpurs and a bushman's shirt with two pockets, she was wearing a belt of beautifully plaited kangaroo hide with three pouches like most bushmen carried, one with a knife, another probably a watch and the third, no doubt, matches. She left as suddenly as she came. 'Gypsy' the mailman said her husband called her.

It fitted her perfectly. I wondered how old she was — perhaps twenty-five. I was cleaning my saddle and oiling it up in readiness for the coming horse muster when Ellison walked in announcing, 'We'll have a cup of tea and get away. We'll be camping out. It'll take a couple of days to muster the horses up.'

I was allotted three saddle horses. A big rangy grey, a good-looking chestnut and another bay with a beautiful head. I saddled the grey which Ellison said was very comfortable to ride. There is a wide range of comfort with saddle horses and not all have a comfortable gait. We were soon on our way with Ellison, his wife and I riding out in the lead and two Aboriginal horse tailers bringing the spare saddle horses and packs along behind.

As we rode, Ellison gave me a rundown on the

station. It was about eleven hundred square miles he said, pointing to a distant range which was roughly his western boundary. Two creeks came down from the mountains forming an approximate boundary, converging about thirty odd miles to the east and forming a triangle. Hence the station's name.

He had owned it, he told me, for going on seven years. It was very run down when he bought it, the cattle were out of hand, and the blacks had been having a great time spearing stock. 'It didn't take long to put a stop to that,' he said, patting a heavy Colt revolver strapped to the pommel of his saddle. 'Mind you, they still get the odd beast but I've got old McNally out there track riding and that keeps them in check.' I nodded, 'Is he the one who's s'posed to dream what's going to happen?' He laughed, 'Yes, but I don't take much account of his dreaming. An odd character, but it doesn't worry me so long as he keeps track riding.' We didn't stop for a dinner camp and after riding seven hours we came to a set of stockyards on a ridge by a creek, where we made camp. Next morning we were up at 'piccaninny daylight'. The Aboriginal horse tailers had the horses ready and we saddled them as the sun was rising. We took Jackson, one of our horse tailers, for tracking purposes. They have superb eyesight and as trackers they have no peer.

We had ridden about five miles when Jackson pulled up and pointed to horse tracks. 'They won't be far from here. This is their feeding ground,' Ellison said, adding as we dismounted to tighten our saddle girths, 'they'll give us a hard gallop.' Looking at his wife he said, 'You're the lightest. When we catch up with them you take the lead, Tom can back you up, Jackson and I will try and keep them together. If they split up they could give us a lot of trouble.' We rode on quietly for another mile then, topping a ridge, we saw fifteen or so horses feeding quietly on a plain. The wind was blowing towards us. 'Couldn't be better,' Ellison whispered as we rode towards them. One suddenly threw up its head, then the rest looked up too and in a flash they were in full gallop.

Mrs Ellison gathered up her reins as her horse got into its stride. It knew what to do. I followed her and we thundered down the hillside, Ellison and Jackson behind me. I was keeping a strong hold on my horse who was fighting for its head. The horses had a lead of several hundred yards but we were cutting that down fast. They were headed for a tree-lined gully and hardly touched it as they flew over. I watched Mrs Ellison, lying along her horse's neck with a strong grip of the reins. Her mount shortened its stride as it prepared to take the gully, but the edge of the creek must have given. They both disappeared in a cloud of dust.

I pulled my horse up on the edge. Mrs Ellison got to her feet covered in dust but unhurt. Her horse was lying on its side floundering and as it struggled to stand, one foreleg swung loosely, broken below the knee. Mrs Ellison gave a pitiful cry and put an arm round its neck. Ellison rode up, took in the situation at a glance and walked towards the horse, his revolver in his hand. Mrs Ellison ran behind a tree, tears streaming down her face, covering her ears as she said, 'Be quick.' It was an awful moment. I held the reins as Ellison put the revolver to the animal's head. A beautiful horse flopped to the ground, dead.

It was a sad procession that made its way back to the camp with Mrs Ellison on Jackson's horse. He walked, carrying his saddle. The next morning we had to make a fresh start, but at least we knew where to look. I didn't see the boss's wife. He and I went out with both the horse tailers, Jackson and Willie. We picked up the tracks again and didn't have to ride too far before we found the mob. They galloped away. Ellison took the lead, I rode behind him and after a short chase we rounded them up. Once we steadied them they didn't give us any trouble and we brought them back to our camp and yarded them.

The next day, on the way back to the station, they trotted along quietly with our horses, giving no trouble. The following morning, Ellison and his wife and I were sitting up on the rails as the horses were being drafted through by the stockmen. There were a few brood mares and a few working horses among about nine youngsters for me to break in. A slashing-looking chestnut came through and Ellison looked at his wife and she nodded. He turned to me and said, 'That's one of my wife's horses. She breaks her own in.' It looked as though I was going to have company in the breaking yard. When drafting was finished I got the breaking gear ready. I was given Jackson as an offsider.

At daylight a day later, I was over at the yard as the horses were brought up. A grey filly and a bay were the first two into the round yard where the breaking was done. First come first served. I dropped a rope over the filly's head, got the tackle on her and roped the other one and soon had it in hand.

I was totally engrossed in my work when I noticed Mrs Ellison sitting upon the top rail. I nodded to her and went on with what I was doing. I supposed that she was going to make a start on the chestnut colt. There were still a few horses in the back of the yard. Among them was a rakish looking grey which she was eyeing speculatively. I took it to be one of the station working horses. Suddenly she said, 'What about giving that grey a ride Tom.'

It didn't seem to be the kind of horse she would ride, a very ordinary run-of-the-mill stock horse — and I didn't like its head much either. You can tell a lot from a horses's head. Nonetheless, I was flattered by the request. I realised afterwards of course, that I walked into it with my eyes open. The horse laid its ears back as I slipped the bridle over its head, a sure sign of a bad temper, but I still didn't wake up. I tightened the girths, took a firm grip of the reins and swung into the saddle, catching a glimpse of the boss's wife with an impish grin on her face as it started to buck. And could it buck! It unleashed a dozen coiled springs as it went up in the air and twisted and I knew I had been caught — I was absolutely furious, I could have strangled the bitch. My shoulder was painful where I hit the ground but my ego was in a worse state.

Most stations have an outlaw somewhere in a back paddock which is never taken into the stock camp because it's too much of a time waster. But if someone comes along and wants to prove something, there's always time for a buckjump show. It's bad manners though, to put someone on a horse like that without telling them — very bad manners. The grey trotted around the yard snorting.

I expect Mrs Ellison saw the murderous mood I was in and it might have scared her. She jumped down off the rail and ran over to me and put both her hands on my shoulders. 'I'm sorry Tom, I shouldn't have done that to you.' All my pent-up fury disappeared instantly and I was her slave from then on. I was still upset, but I expect that was my ego.

Later, when I looked back on the incident and could laugh, she told me that the outlaw had never been ridden. It was one of those horses that was unrideable. Apparently Ellison had been talking about selling it to a buckjump show where he could have got a good price for it, but never got around to it.

The following day Mrs Ellison was working her colt in an adjoining yard in a very competent manner. She had the mouthing tackle on it and let it walk around to get used to the feel of the gear. I was sitting up on the rail watching a couple of mine being worked by Jackson. She climbed up and joined me. 'Your colt should be ready to ride tomorrow,' I said.

'Yes,' she agreed, 'I'll ride him out with you,' Then smiling she added, 'Call me Gypsy, Tom.'

For a minute or two I was too embarrassed to answer and just mumbled 'Yes, Mrs Ellison.'

'Go on, say yes, Gypsy', smiling mischievously.

'Yes, Gypsy, thank you.'

I think I was going the colour of a beetroot. I was relieved when she jumped down off the rail and went back to her horse. Ellison walked down to the yard to ask how the breaking was going and I pointed out a bay colt with a blaze and told him that it would be above average. Gypsy left her colt with the stockman who was helping her and went up to the house with her husband.

The next day Gypsy was at the yard first and already had the chestnut saddled. I had three to ride out and I saddled a bay filly. We rode out together. Her colt behaved beautifully and I congratulated her on the job she'd done. When we returned to the yard she said, 'I'll give you a hand to ride one of yours, Tom.' I was happy to hear her say that. Apart from her company it was something that I was getting paid for.

We saddled up and rode out to a creek two or three miles away where there was a beautiful waterhole shaded by huge gum trees. Our horses drank deeply and when they were finished I tethered them in the shade and began taking the saddles off to allow them to cool off. Gypsy walked down to the water's edge and suddenly I heard a loud splash from the waterhole. It quite startled me and looking over my shoulder I saw Gypsy surfacing with an impish grin on her face. Her clothes were flung carelessly over a bush. 'Come on in, Tom,' she called, 'it's beautiful.'

I don't think the *Guinness Book of Records* was in existence then but had it been I would have had a permanent spot for the speed with which I got my clothes off.

Each day we were riding further, each day we were staying out longer. Her husband didn't seem to mind. In a half-grumbling way he said to me, 'Can't keep her away from horses.' It was the day that I told him I needed some more youngsters and he said, 'Right, we'll do a muster tomorrow.' As it turned out it was the day after. Riding along he said, 'We'll go to McNally's camp first, he'll know where the horses we want are running.' Gypsy said, 'I don't like him, he gives me the creeps.' Mark laughed, 'He's certainly gone a bit strange lately. I think it goes with the job, most boundary riders are a bit mad. I suppose being out on their own, talking to themselves, they all get that way.' I asked him about McNally's dreaming and again he dismissed it. 'I don't take any notice of that.'

We reached the boundary rider's camp but he wasn't there so we took a sweep around looking for tracks. I rode away in one direction with Jackson and Mark and his wife went in another. After riding for a short time we came across tracks which Jackson said were some of the horses we wanted — there were eight sets altogether.

It did not take long to catch up with them. They gave us a hard gallop for a mile or so but after a while they steadied down and once we swung them they gave us no trouble. Just before we headed them I felt my horse falter, then he picked up again and kept going. I knew he had hurt himself. When we had them rounded up I dismounted and examined my horse's foot. He was bleeding from the off-side coronet.

Shortly after, Mark and his wife galloped up with another mob and after Mark examined my horse's foot he said, 'You stay here and watch this lot. My wife can stay too — her horse is just about buggered. I'll take Jackson with me.'

They rode away and as the horses were feeding quietly we dismounted. We were sitting on a fallen tree chatting away when my horse suddenly threw up its head and I looked round to see what had startled him. I saw a single horseman approaching. Gypsy stood up and whispered to me, 'It's McNally.' He rode up looking me up and down, 'G'day missus.' She nodded and said, 'This is Tom Cole, our breaker.'

A gaunt-looking man, with a prominent hooked nose, he looked like some predatory bird, sitting on his horse eyeing us. Gypsy seemed very ill at ease. Then we heard galloping and Mark and Jackson thundered over the ridge with a mob of horses. The new ones milled around for a while, whinnying, before they settled down and joined the mob.

McNally rode over and spoke briefly to the boss. I heard him say something about marauding blacks and a cow being speared, and that he would be coming in to the station in a day or so to replenish his rations. Then he rode away without another word. We took the horses to a yard where we camped for the night. The next day we returned to the station and the following day drafted the horses. When we were finished there were twelve breakers. Ellison went back to the house, Gypsy went with him and I was on my own with Jackson. It was a long day. The following day was even longer. I caught a brief glimpse of Gypsy in the garden, picking some flowers. I had worked myself up into quite a state.

On the third day she came down as I was saddling a colt. Smiling mischievously she said, 'Did you miss me?'

I turned my back so that she couldn't see my face, tightening a girth with unnecessary force. 'Of course.' Then, 'Which horse shall I ride?' 'Take that brown horse,' I told her, pointing to a youngster that I thought would turn out to be above average. I had already given it a ride and was pleased with the way it had handled.

I told Jackson what to do as we rode away. I was so relieved that Gypsy was back with me that the whole world took on a brighter hue. The birds sang louder than ever and the kookaburras were laughing cheerfully. Riding along she said, 'Tom, you've got to be sensible. It's no good you getting upset if you don't see me for a couple of days.' I immediately saw the commonsense of that and it made me feel better. To say that I was carried away would be an understatement. She was young, she was beautiful, she was a slashing horsewoman, she was bright and stimulating company. She had a husband too and I'd better not lose sight of that I thought.

We came to a creek where we gave the horses a drink and I unsaddled them. We were away for a long time.

I was getting close to the end of the breaking, something that I wasn't looking forward to. But I couldn't stretch it out much longer. On a beautiful morning a couple of days later we rode out together. Gypsy said: 'You must be getting close to finishing the breaking Tom?' 'Yes,' I said miserably, 'there's only four left and they're in tackling.'

We rode along quietly, each with our own thoughts. Then suddenly she gathered up her reins and put her horse into a gallop. I did the same. It was exhilarating. We came to a spring where the water bubbled cool and clear under gums spreading a wide shade. We took the saddles from the horses, tied them

up in the shade and sat down on the bank. Time
galloped away. The sun was getting high and it was
time to return before the heat built up.

I was riding a black horse which, because of his bad
temper, I had called Satan and Gypsy was on a grey I'd
named Silver, a good-looking, free-striding youngster.
She turned to me. 'Tom, I think I'll take this horse into
my string. I'd like to have something to remind me of
you.' I was very deeply touched by this because she
was always so insistent that no one ever broke in a
horse for her.

We were close to home and we gave our horses a
last sprint as the stockyard came into sight. She was
laughing as she beat me to the stockyard gate and we
pulled up in a cloud of dust. One on the boys opened
the gate and I looked up. Sitting on a top rail looking
like some vulture I saw McNally. Gypsy saw him at the
same time and the smile left her face. She threw her
reins to the stockman who had opened the gate, and
walked away without a word.

McNally looked at me with an evil grin. There was
no reason why he shouldn't be there — after all the
man worked at the place — but I was almost in a state
of shock. I think probably my feelings were largely the
result of Gypsy's reaction when she saw him. 'I thought
you'd have finished the breaking a week or so ago,' he
said.

'Well, there was no great hurry,' was all I could
think to reply, as I went to the yard where the horses
were milling around. I made sure they were washed
down before being turned out then I went over to my
quarters, had a shower and made my way to the
kitchen. McNally was already there. He didn't seem to
be much of a conversationalist and I was in no mood to
talk anyway. He obviously had a permanent room in
the quarters to which he retired.

In the morning I was up at my usual time, just before sunrise. After making sure that the horses were in the yard ready for a day's work, I went to the kitchen. McNally joined me a few minutes later. We had our breakfast almost in silence. I tried to make conversation but got not much more than grunts. We left together. He was eyeing me off speculatively as we walked the short distance to our quarters adjacent to the workshop and saddle room. Suddenly he stopped and faced me, his great beak of a nose a few inches from my face. 'I had a dream last night, young fella, I think I oughta tell you about it. The boss shot the horsebreaker.' I was stunned. 'Jesus Christ! You what?' 'I dreamed the boss shot the horsebreaker.' Then he turned and walked away.

I recalled with great clarity that Ellison had shot a man on the goldfields. I walked over to the yard where the horses were waiting to be worked and called to Jackson, 'Get these horses saddled up, we're going to ride them out today.' For the first time I hoped Gypsy wouldn't come down to the yard. The youngsters were pretty green but I knocked them into shape — really forced them. They came to hand fairly well. A couple bucked a bit but they weren't much trouble. Getting them mouthed was the most important thing so that they would turn and stop without too much pressure.

It was late afternoon when I saw Ellison walking down towards the yard. He wasn't carrying any kind of a firearm, I noted with relief. He asked me how the breaking was coming along. I told him that I would be finished that day and I'd like to get away tomorrow. He seemed surprised but didn't comment except to say, 'Very well, I'll have your cheque ready.' I went back to the horses. Never anywhere were colts broken in quicker. After I turned them out I went to the saddle room and got my packs ready. I told Jackson to have my horses mustered up and in the yard at first light.

I spent a restless night and was up before daylight, finished breakfast before McNally showed up and went over to the yard. I knew Ellison would be coming over to give me my cheque. I made sure my rifle, a Winchester .32, was handy. He came down after he'd had his breakfast and asked if any of the horses had any peculiarities. I pointed out the two that would probably buck a bit until they got worked in, a brown horse I'd called Midas and a bay named Jackson. I always named one horse after my offsider. There was another bay, Victor, and a nice little filly, Pussycat.

Ellison seemed pleased with them and told me he thought I'd done a good job. He gave me my cheque and with some nervousness I shook his hand. He went back to the house. I never saw any sign of McNally and didn't want to.

I was packing up when Gypsy walked in. I could see by the look on her face that she knew. We embraced, her cheeks were wet. It was very quick, which was the best way.

She whispered, 'Goodbye' and walked away.

As I rode away I couldn't help thinking of the aptness of the name Triangle. Although it had stunned and upset me, McNally's dreaming, if he *did* dream it, was probably an undisguised blessing. Since then I have thought about it a great deal and come to the conclusion that the whole affair would not have been very difficult to work out. With their unparalleled knowledge of tracking, the Aboriginal stockmen would have had a good idea what was going on from the start. Ellison had shot one man, shooting another one, especially under the circumstances, would be a lot easier.

Tom Cole
Riding the Wildman Plains

From the bestselling author of *Hell West and Crooked*
comes another outback classic.

At seventeen, Tom Cole left England, lured by the
posters that beckoned young empire builders to the
colonies. He arrived to a harsh, unyielding and alien
land. Australia.

Twenty-five years later, Tom Cole was an outback
legend.

Famed as an expert horseman and a skilled crocodile
and buffalo hunter, Tom lived a life most people only
dream about. Now, thanks to Tom's mother in England
who kept all his letters, and to the diaries Tom wrote to
keep track of the days, we have a unique and
remarkable record of what his day-to-day life was really
like.

Written with laconic easy-going humour, the diaries and
letters bring to life outback Australia in the thirties and
forties. Illustrated with Tom's own photographs as well
as maps and reproductions of his letters and diaries,
Riding the Wildman Plains tells of a time and a breed of
pioneering bushman that will never be seen again.

'Forget Crocodile Dundee — here is a person who rode
down enraged buffaloes with his horse, picking them off
with one-handed rifle shots as the herd charged for his
mount.'
COURIER MAIL

'He records his remarkable life story in a part of
Australian that for most of us might as well be a foreign
country ... His memories and yarns preserve an era that
we will never see in Australia again.'
CANBERRA TIMES